Soul Cry

Powerful Prayers from the Spiritual Heritage of African Americans

HONOR IB BOOKS

Inspiration and Motivation for the Seasons of Life

COOK COMMUNICATIONS MINISTRIES
Colorado Springs, Colorado • Paris, Ontario
KINGSWAY COMMUNICATIONS LTD
Eastbourne, England

Honor Books® is an imprint of
Cook Communications Ministries, Colorado Springs, Colorado 80918
Cook Communications, Paris, Ontario
Kingsway Communications Ltd, Eastbourne, England

SOUL CRY—POWERFUL PRAYERS FROM THE SPIRITUAL HERITAGE OF
AFRICAN AMERICANS
© 2004 by BORDON BOOKS

First printing, 2004
Printed in the United States of America
  3 4 5 6 Printing/Year 08 07 06 05 04

Developed by Bordon Books
Manuscript written by Ronald C. Jordan.
Cover designed by Koechel Peterson & Associates.

Note: Some texts have been updated for today's readers.

ISBN: 1-56292-339-0

Presented to:

Renee'

From:

Linda

Date:

August , 2008

—ɯ—

INTRODUCTION

As African Americans, we have reason to be proud of our culture and heritage. Not only is our culture rich in tradition and history, but the people who came before us lived lives that were rich in a faith born out of perseverance under great difficulty. Previous generations passed a legacy to us of a people whose God listens to their prayers, and we'll want to pass it on to our children, our friends, and our neighbors.

Through the crucible of affliction, depth and substance are forged. *Soul Cry—Powerful Prayers from the Spiritual Heritage of African Americans* is a collection of powerful prayers of African Americans past and present that will kindle a desire in you to touch the heart of God. This prayerful wisdom of generations will touch your heart, move your spirit, and inspire your own communication with God.

This amazing collection also includes a topical section of contemporary prayers for your daily needs. You will find yourself adding your own "Amen" with each turn of the page.

COURAGE FOR WHAT IS RIGHT

One isn't necessarily born with courage,
but one is born with potential. Without courage,
we cannot practice any other virtue with consistency.
We can't be kind, true, merciful, generous, or honest.

MAYA ANGELOU

HE WHO DWELLS IN THE SHELTER OF THE MOST HIGH WILL ABIDE
IN THE SHADOW OF THE ALMIGHTY. I WILL SAY TO THE LORD,
"MY REFUGE AND MY FORTRESS, MY GOD, IN WHOM I TRUST!"

PSALM 91:1-2 NASB

You are the great God of all the earth and the heavens.

We are so insignificant.

In us there are many defects.

But the power is yours to make and to do what we cannot do.

You know all about us.

For coming down to earth you were despised

and mocked, and brutally treated

because of the same defects in the men of those days.

For those men you prayed,

because they did not understand what they were doing.

You came only for what was right.

Give us the courage to struggle in the same way for what is right.

O Lord, help us who roam about.

Help us who have been placed in Africa and

have no dwelling place of our own.

Give us a dwelling place. O God, all power is yours

in heaven and earth. Amen.

CHIEF HOSEA KUTAKO, *A Prayer from Africa*

A THANKFUL HEART

God gave you a gift of 86,400 seconds today.

Have you used one to say thank you?

WILLIAM A. WARD

NOT THAT I SPEAK IN REGARD TO NEED, FOR I HAVE

LEARNED IN WHATEVER STATE I AM, TO BE CONTENT.

PHILIPPIANS 4:11 NKJV

Soul Cry

I thank You God for letting me see

another beautiful day with You

Thank You for letting me hear the birds sing

forgiving me of all bad things

Thank You for Your gentle touch

in all my troubles it means so much

Thank You for letting me feel the cool breeze

and for not counting all my bad deeds

Thank You for the fresh smell of rain

and easing all my heartaches and pains

Thank You God for loving me

Your Humble Servant, Georgia Lee

GEORGIA L. GORDON

SOJOURNERS

I have no protection at home nor resting place abroad.
I am an outcast from the society of my childhood, and
an outlaw in the land of my birth. I am a stranger
with thee and all my fathers were sojourners.

FREDERICK DOUGLASS, *My Bondage and My Freedom*

THE LORD IS FAITHFUL, AND HE WILL STRENGTHEN
[YOU] *and* SET YOU ON A FIRM FOUNDATION
AND GUARD YOU FROM THE EVIL [ONE].

2 THESSALONIANS 3:3 AMP

God of our weary years,
God of our silent tears,
Thou hast brought us thus far on the way.

Thou who has by Thy might
Led us into the light,
Keep us forever in the path, we pray;

Lest our feet stray from the places, our God, where we met Thee,
Lest our hearts drunk with the wine of the world, we forget Thee.

Shadowed beneath Thy hand,

May we forever stand,

True to our God, true to our native land!

JAMES WELDON JOHNSON

———∿∿∿———

I WILL LOOK UP TO THEE!

Go within every day and find the inner strength
so that the world will not blow your candle out.[1]

KATHERINE DUNHAM

GOD IS OUR REFUGE AND STRENGTH

[MIGHTY AND IMPENETRABLE TO TEMPTATION],

A VERY PRESENT AND WELL-PROVED HELP IN TROUBLE.

PSALM 46:1 AMP

I will look up to Thee

With faith's ne'er-failing sight,

My trust repose in Thee,
Though dark and chill earth's night.

I will look up to Thee,
Though rough and long the way,
Still sure Thou leadest me
Unto the perfect day.

I will look up to Thee
When lone and faint and weak.
"My grace sufficeth Thee;"
I hear Thy soft voice speak.

I will look up to Thee,
For if Thou, Lord, art near,
Temptations quickly flee,
And clouds soon disappear.

I will look up to Thee
With feeble voice I cry.
Lord, pity helpless me—
Without Thy aid I die.

I will look up to Him
Who died my soul to save;
Who bore my load of sin—
His blood a ransom gave.

Soul Cry

I will look up to Thee,
The all-anointed one,
Who opens the gate for me,
To the eternal throne.

I will look up to Thee;
I feel my sins forgiven—
Thy footprints, Lord, I see,
They mark the way to Heaven.

I will look up to Thee,
When doubt and fear arise;
Though dangers compass me,
Upward I lift mine eyes.

I will look up to Thee,
Who knoweth all my needs;
Thy spirit, Lord, grant me,
My soul in anguish leads.

I will look up to Thee!
Though all I have below,
Thou takest, Lord, from me,
Thou canst the more bestow.

I will look up to Thee,
Thou bright and morning star;

Soul Cry

With eyes of faith I see,
Thy glory from afar.

I will look up to Thee,
My hand shall rest in Thine;
Where e'er Thou wilt lead me,
Thy will, O Lord, not mine!

I will look up to Thee,
When death's relentless hand,
Has laid its weight on me,
Save—Thou atoning Lamb!

I will look up to Thee,
When crossing Jordan's wave;
Then, Lord, I look to Thee—
Whose power alone can save!

JOSEPHINE HERD

I CAN FLY!

I can come when I please
I can go when I please
I can flit, fly and flutter,
Like the birds in the trees.

ETHEL WATERS, *His Eye Is on the Sparrow*, 1925

CHRIST HAS SET US FREE TO LIVE A FREE LIFE.
SO TAKE YOUR STAND! NEVER AGAIN LET
ANYONE PUT A HARNESS OF SLAVERY ON YOU.

GALATIANS 5:1 MSG

When the time came for us to go to bed, we all knelt down in family prayer, as was our custom; father's prayer seemed more real to me that night than ever before, especially in the words,

"Lord, hasten the time when these children shall be their own free men and women."

My faith in father's prayer made me think that the Lord would answer him at the farthest in two or three weeks, but it was fully six years before it came and father had been dead two years before the war.[2]

JACOB STROYER, *My Life in the South,* 1898

—꜃—

MY HOPE IS IN THEE

As I reflect down the vistas of the past, as I think about
all the problems and all the experiences I have had;
without a faith in God, a faith in prayer, and a disposition
of loyalty to God, I don't know what I would have done.

REV. C. L. FRANKLIN, "HANNA, THE IDEAL MOTHER," 1958

LEAN ON, TRUST IN, *and* BE CONFIDENT IN THE LORD
WITH ALL YOUR HEART *and* MIND AND DO NOT
RELY ON YOUR OWN INSIGHT *or* UNDERSTANDING.

PROVERBS 3:5 AMP

O Thou King eternal, immortal, invisible, and only wise God, before whom angels bow and seraphs veil their faces, crying holy,

holy, holy, is the Lord God Almighty. True and righteous are Thy ways, Thou King of saints. Help me, Thy poor unworthy creature, humbly to prostrate myself before Thee, and implore that mercy which my sins have justly forfeited.

O God, I know that I am not worthy of a place at Thy footstool; but to whom shall I go but unto Thee? Thou alone hast the words of eternal life. Send me not away without a blessing, I beseech Thee; but enable me to wrestle like Jacob, and to prevail like Israel. Be graciously pleased, O God, to pardon all that Thou hast seen amiss in me this day, and enable me to live more to Thine honor and glory for the time to come. Bless the church to which I belong, and grant that when Thou makest up Thy jewels, not one soul shall be found missing.

Bless him in whom Thou hast set over us as a watchman in Zion. Let not his soul be discouraged. May he not fail to declare the whole counsel of God, whether sinners will hear or forbear.

And now, Lord, what wait I for? My hope is in Thee. Do more for me than I can possibly ask or think, and finally receive me to Thyself.

MARIA W. STEWART

NOT BY JUSTICE, BUT BY GRACE

There comes a time when a cup of endurance runs over, and men
are no longer willing to be plunged into an abyss of injustice,
where they experience the blackness of corroding despair.

MARTIN LUTHER KING JR.

"I HAVE COME THAT THEY MAY HAVE LIFE,
AND HAVE IT TO THE FULL."

JOHN 10:10 NIV

Dear Lord, I am bewildered by the angry world.
I do not know the meaning of the flags unfurled.
The noisy skies, the tortured seas;
What sayest Thou, O Lord, to these?

I hear the strident call to arms; above the scenes
Of men in desperate debate; their war machines
Defile the skies, pollute the earth.
How much, O Lord, can peace be worth?

Hast Thou in merited disgust turned back from man
Who recklessly has broken trust and sinned again?

Forgive our selfish lust for power
And save us in this dreadful hour.

Return, O Lord, return and save this wretched race,
Save us, not by Thy justice, Lord, but grace,
Forgive our foolish, pompous way,
And save us from ourselves, we pray.[3]

CHARLES ERIC LINCOLN, PH.D., 1944

SET US FREE!

*All the nations of the earth are crying out for liberty and equality.
Away, away with tyranny and oppression! And shall Africa's sons
be silent any longer? Far be it from me to recommend to you either
to kill, burn, or destroy. But I would strongly recommend to you to
improve your talents; let not one lie buried in the earth. Show forth
your powers of mind. Prove to the world that though black your
skins as shades of night, your hearts are pure, your souls are white.*

MARIA W. STEWART

NOW, LORD, CONSIDER THEIR THREATS AND ENABLE YOUR

SERVANTS TO SPEAK YOUR WORD WITH GREAT BOLDNESS.

ACTS 4:29 NIV

Set us free, O heavenly Father, from every bond of prejudice

and fear: that, honoring the steadfast courage of Your servants

Absalom Jones and Richard Allen, we may show forth in our lives

the reconciling love and true freedom of the children of God, which

You have given us in our Savior Jesus Christ, who lives and reigns

with You and the Holy Spirit, one God, now and forever.

ABSALOM JONES

LORD, GIVE US PEACE!

*Public peace is the act of public trust, it is the faith
that all are secure and will remain secure.*

RICHARD WRIGHT, NATIVE SON, 1940

THEN THEY WILL HAMMER THEIR SWORDS INTO
PLOWSHARES AND THEIR SPEARS INTO PRUNING HOOKS;
NATION WILL NOT LIFT UP SWORD AGAINST NATION,
AND NEVER AGAIN WILL THEY TRAIN FOR WAR.

MICAH 4:3 NASB

Lord God of Hosts, incline Your ear
To this, Your humble servant's prayer:
May war and strife and discord cease;
This century, Lord God, give us peace!
Henceforth, dear Lord, may we abhor
Thought of strife, the curse of war.
One blessing more, our store increase,
This is our prayer, Lord, give us peace!

May those who rule us rule with love,
As You do rule the courts above;

Soul Cry

May man to man as brothers feel,
Lay down their arms and quit the field;
Change from our brows the angry looks,
Turn swords and spears to pruning hooks.
One blessing more our store increase,
This is our prayer, Lord, give us peace!

May flags of war fore'er be furled,
The milk white flag wave o'er the world;
Let not a slave be heard to cry,
Lion and lamb together lie;
May nations meet in one accord
Around one peaceful festive board.
One blessing more, our store increase,
This is our prayer, Lord, give us peace!

JOSEPH EPHRAIM MCGIRT, *The Century Prayer*

ALL YOUR GIFTS

*To be a poor man is hard, but to be a poor race in
a land of dollars is the very bottom of hardship.*

W. E. B. DuBois, *The Souls of Black Folk*

THEN WE, YOUR PEOPLE, THE ONES YOU LOVE AND
CARE FOR, WILL THANK YOU OVER AND OVER
AND OVER. WE'LL TELL EVERYONE WE MEET HOW
WONDERFUL YOU ARE, HOW PRAISEWORTHY YOU ARE!

PSALM 79:13 MSG

Great God, accept our gratitude,
For the great gifts on us bestowed—
For raiment, shelter and for food.

Great God, our gratitude we bring,
Accept our humble offering,
For all the gifts on us bestowed,
Thy name be evermore adored.[4]

JOSEPHINE DELPHINE HENDERSON, 1901

FEED MY SHEEP

Jesus said, "If you love me, feed my sheep."
I want to feed the sheep.

MELBA MOORE

WHATEVER YOUR HAND FINDS TO DO,

DO IT WITH ALL YOUR MIGHT.

ECCLESIASTES 9:10 NIV

God, my hands are small,

but I can help in many ways.

My legs are not long,

but I can run an errand for an elderly or sick neighbor who can't.

My voice is not as loud as others,

but I can sing a soothing melody and cheer a heart.

Thank You, God, for making me useful.[5]

MARIAN WRIGHT EDELMAN, *I'm Your Child, God: Prayers for Our Children*

HELP US TO WALK TOGETHER

*Commitment means that it is possible for a man to yield
the nerve center of his consent to a purpose or cause,
a movement or an ideal, which may be more
important to him than whether he lives or dies.*

HOWARD THURMAN, DISCIPLINES OF THE SPIRIT, 1963

COMMIT THY WAY UNTO THE LORD; TRUST ALSO IN HIM;
AND HE SHALL BRING IT TO PASS.

PSALM 37:5 KJV

O God, our heavenly Father, we thank Thee for this golden
privilege to worship Thee, the only true God of the universe. We
come to Thee today grateful that Thou hast kept us through the
long night of the past and ushered us into the challenge of the
present and the bright hope of the future. We are mindful, O God,
that man cannot save himself, for man is not the measure of things,
and humanity is not God.

Bound by our chains of sin and finiteness, we know we need a
savior. We thank Thee, O God, for the spiritual nature of man. We
are in nature, but we live above nature. Help us never to let anyone

or any condition pull us so low as to cause us to hate. Give us the strength to love our enemies and do good to those who despitefully use us and persecute us.

We thank Thee for Thy Church, founded upon the Word, that challenges us to do more than sing and pray, but go out and work as though the very answer to our prayers depended on us and not upon Thee. Then, finally, help us to realize that man was created to shine like the stars and live on through all eternity.

Keep us, we pray, in perfect peace; help us to walk together, pray together, sing together, and live together until that day when all of God's children—Black, White, Red, and Yellow—will rejoice in one common band of humanity in the kingdom of our Lord and of our God, we pray. Amen.[6]

REV. HAROLD A. CARTER, *The Prayer Tradition of Black People*

I Rejoice

Having God for my friend and portion, what have I to fear?
As long as it is the will of God, I rejoice that I am as I am;
for man, in his best estate, is altogether vanity.

Maria Stewart, *Meditations from the Pen of Mrs. Maria W. Stewart,* 1879

Be strong and of good courage, do not fear for
the LORD your God, he is the One who goes with you;
he will not leave you, nor forsake you.

Deuteronomy 31:6 NKJV

O Lord God, as the heavens are high above the earth, so are Your ways above our ways, and Your thoughts above our thoughts. For wise and holy purposes best known to Yourself, You have seen fit to deprive me of all earthly relatives; but when my father and mother forsook me, then You did take me up.

I desire to thank You, that I am this day a living witness to testify that You are a God that will ever vindicate the cause of the poor and needy, and that You have always proved Yourself to be a friend and father to me. O, continue Your lovingkindness even unto the end; and when health and strength begin to decay, and I, as it were, draw nigh unto the grave, O then afford me Your heart-cheering presence, and enable me to rely entirely upon You.

Never leave me nor forsake me, but have mercy upon me for Your great name's sake. And not for myself alone do I ask these blessings, but for all the poor and needy, all widows and fatherless children, for the stranger in distress; and may they call upon You in such manner as to be convinced that You are a prayer-hearing and prayer-answering God; and Yours shall be the praise, forever. Amen.

MARIA W. STEWART, *A Prayer for Divine Companionship* (1835)

—⚊⚊—

GRACE TO DARE MIGHTY CAUSES

Persistence and a positive attitude are necessary ingredients for any successful venture.

L. DOUGLASS WILDER

FIGHT THE GOOD FIGHT OF FAITH.

1 TIMOTHY 6:12 KJV

Give us grace, O God, to dare to do the deed

which we well know cries to be done.

Let us not hesitate because of ease, or the

words of men's mouths, or our own lives.

Mighty causes are calling us—the freeing of women,

the training of children, the putting down of hate

and murder and poverty—all these and more.

But they call with voices that mean work and sacrifice and death.

Mercifully grant us, O God, the spirit of Esther, that we may say:

I will go unto the King and if I perish, I perish.

Amen.

W. E. B. Du Bois, *Prayers for Dark People*

—⁓—

Let My Soul Be Free

In His good time America shall rend the Veil, and
the prisoned shall go free. Free, free as the sunshine
trickling down the morning into these high windows . . .
free as yonder fresh young voices welling up to me from the
caverns of brick and mortar below—swelling with song.

W. E. B. Du Bois

Soul Cry

AND THE CHIEF CAPTAIN ANSWERED,
WITH A GREAT SUM OBTAINED I THIS FREEDOM.
ACTS 22:28 KJV

Through my degradations
And my tribulations
My lynchings and my weariness
Let my soul be free
Lead me toward the norther light
Protect me from Mastas spite
Create in me a temple of glee
I shall be set free
Towards the light beaten and torn
I will still crawl
For this is no free-for-all
Dear Lord, let my soul be free
With freedom I shall be a better man
Will you grab this outreached hand
So I can protect my fellow woman
And raise my offspring free
No mo disrespect
No mo lynchings
No mo hard work and muscle flinches
I breath just to be free

Pass me a sign
Nothing of complicated design
I will do all it takes for me and my people to be free.

JAY HORNE, *A Slave's Prayer*

JESUS, WALK WITH ME

Courage is the determination not to be overwhelmed by any object, that power of the mind capable of sloughing off the thingification of the past.

MARTIN LUTHER KING JR.

YE SHALL NOT NEED TO FIGHT IN THIS BATTLE: SET YOURSELVES, STAND YE STILL, AND SEE THE SALVATION OF THE LORD WITH YOU, O JUDAH AND JERUSALEM: FEAR NOT, NOR BE DISMAYED; TOMORROW GO OUT AGAINST THEM: FOR THE LORD WILL BE WITH YOU.

2 CHRONICLES 20:17 KJV

I want Jesus to walk with me,
I want Jesus to walk with me,
All along my pilgrim journey,
Lord, I want Jesus to walk with me.

In my trials, Lord, walk with me,
In my trials, Lord, walk with me,
When the shades of life are falling,
Lord, I want Jesus to walk with me.

I Want Jesus to Walk with Me, AFRICAN-AMERICAN SPIRITUAL

—⁓⁓—

THY GRACIOUS BALM I NEED

*Mankind must realize that it is in need of healing,
not from the outer world, but from within.*

CAROLYN WARFIELD, *Rising to the Light Within*

GO UP INTO GILEAD, AND TAKE BALM, O VIRGIN,
THE DAUGHTER OF EGYPT: IN VAIN SHALT THOU USE
MANY MEDICINES; FOR THOU SHALT NOT BE CURED.

JEREMIAH 46:11 KJV

O LORD, the hard-won miles
Have worn my stumbling feet:
Oh, soothe me with Thy smiles,
And make my life complete.

The thorns were thick and keen
Where'er I trembling trod;
The way was long between
My wounded feet and God.

Where healing waters flow
Do thou my footsteps lead.
My heart is aching so;
Thy gracious balm I need.

LET US JOIN TOGETHER

*In all things purely social we can be as separate
as the five fingers, and yet one as the hand
in all things essential to mutual purpose.*

BOOKER T. WASHINGTON

Soul Cry

"COME NOW, LET US ARGUE THIS OUT," SAYS THE LORD.
"NO MATTER HOW DEEP THE STAIN OF YOUR SINS,
I CAN REMOVE IT. I CAN MAKE YOU AS CLEAN AS
FRESHLY FALLEN SNOW. EVEN IF YOU ARE STAINED AS
RED AS CRIMSON, I CAN MAKE YOU AS WHITE AS WOOL."

ISAIAH 1:18 NLT

Oh God, help us in our lives and in all of our attitudes,
to work out this controlling force of love,
this controlling power that can solve
every problem that we confront in all areas.
Oh, we talk about politics;
we talk about the problems facing our atomic civilization.
Grant that all men will come together and discover
that as we solve the crisis and solve these problems,
the international problems,
the problems of atomic energy,
the problems of nuclear energy,
and yes, even the race problem;
let us join together in a great fellowship of love
and bow down at the feet of Jesus.
Give us this strong determination.
In the name and spirit of this Christ, we pray Amen.

DR. MARTIN LUTHER KING JR., 1957

FIX MY HEART

If you lose hope, somehow you lose the vitality that keeps life moving, you lose that courage to be, that quality that helps you go on in spite of it all. And so today I still have a dream.

MARTIN LUTHER KING JR.

CREATE IN ME A CLEAN HEART, O GOD;
AND RENEW A RIGHT SPIRIT WITHIN ME.

PSALM 51:10 KJV

Give me a clean heart
So I may serve Thee.
Lord, fix my heart
So that I may be used by Thee.
Lord, I'm not worthy of all these blessings.
Give me a clean heart, and I'll follow Thee.

—◊◊◊—

HELP THIS PRECIOUS CHILD

TRAIN UP A CHILD IN THE WAY HE SHOULD GO,
EVEN WHEN HE IS OLD HE WILL NOT DEPART FROM IT.

PROVERBS 22:6 NASB

Dear God, I thank You for the gift of this child to raise,

this life to share, this mind to help mold,

this body to nurture, and this spirit to enrich.

Let me never betray this child's trust, dampen this

child's hope, or discourage this child's dreams.

Help me, dear God, to help this precious child

become all You mean him to be.

Let Your grace and love fall on him like gentle breezes and give him

inner strength and peace and patience for the journey ahead.

MARIAN WRIGHT EDELMAN

ONLY FROM GOD

To dedicate oneself to the highest good that he knows,
to hold on to the highest ideals that he knows, and to
never compromise certain principles—reward and victory
and success may be slow for you, but victory is surely yours
if you do not allow your spirit, your ambition, your faith
to be destroyed under the impact of trials and crises.

REV. C. L. FRANKLIN

IT IS NOT THAT WE THINK WE CAN DO
ANYTHING OF LASTING VALUE BY OURSELVES.
OUR ONLY POWER AND SUCCESS COME FROM GOD.

2 CORINTHIANS 3:5 NLT

O Lord God, Paul may plant, and Apollos water, but You alone give the increase. We are sensible that without You we can do nothing. Vain are all our efforts without Your blessing. But, O Lord God, You have the hearts of all Your creatures in hand; and You can turn them whithersoever You will.

Strip the hearts of this people from their idols, we humbly beseech You. Take off their eyes from beholding vanity. You can glorify Yourself in making them the monuments of Your mercy; and You canst glorify Yourself in making them the monuments of Your wrath.

Glorify Yourself in making them the monuments of Your victorious grace. Open their eyes that they may see that their feet stand upon slippery places and that fiery billows roll beneath them. And, O Lord God, will You in an especial manner have mercy on our unconverted brethren. Soften their proud and rebellious hearts, and be not angry with them forever.

O, Jesus of Nazareth, have You not died that they might become live? Have You not become poor, that they might become rich? Is not Your blood sufficient to atone? Wherefore, O Lord God, have You hardened their hearts, and blinded their eyes? Wherefore have You so long withheld from them the divine influences of Your Holy Spirit?

Open their eyes that they may see that they are going down to hell, as fast as the wheels of time can carry them. O, stop them in their mad career! Grant that a grievous cry might be heard among Your professing children, in behalf of perishing souls; and may it be like the cry of the Egyptians in the night that You did slay their firstborn.

And not only for ourselves do we pray, but for all nations, kindreds, tongues and people. Grant that an innumerable host, which no one can number, may be gathered in from the four winds of heaven. And when the last trumpet shall sound, grant that we may be caught up into the cloud of the air, and ear saluted with the joyful sound, "Well done, thou good and faithful servant; you have been faithful over a few things, I will make you ruler over many things; enter into the joy of your Lord.[7]

MARIA W. STEWART

—◆—

AT YOUR CALL HUMANITY SPRANG FORTH!

It shall flash through coming ages,
It shall light the distant years;
And eyes now dim with sorrow
Shall be bright through the years.

FRANCES E. W. HARPER, EMANCIPATION PROCLAMATION, © 1865

HOW PRECIOUS IS YOUR LOVINGKINDNESS, O GOD! AND THE CHILDREN OF MEN TAKE REFUGE IN THE SHADOW OF YOUR WINGS.

PSALM 36:7 NASB

Oh, God!

We thank You, that You did condescend to listen to the
cries of Africa's wretched sons; and that You did
interfere in their behalf. At Your call humanity sprang
forth, and espoused the cause of the oppressed; one
hand she employed in drawing from their vitals the
deadly arrows of injustice; and the other in holding a
shield to defend them from fresh assaults; and at that
illustrious moment when the sons of '76 pronounced
these United States free and independent; when the
spirit of patriotism erected a temple sacred to liberty;
when the inspired voices of Americans first uttered those
noble sentiments, "We hold these truths to be self-
evident, that all men are created equal; that they are
endowed by their Creator with certain unalienable
rights; among which are life, liberty, and the pursuit of
happiness"; and when the bleeding African, lifting his
fetters exclaimed, "Am I not a man and a brother?"; then
with redoubled efforts, the angel of humanity strove to
restore to the African race the inherent rights of man.

PETER WILLIAMS JR., 1808

—⟋⟍—

O That I Were Free!

O Freedom! Freedom! Oh, how oft
Thy loving children call on thee!
In wailings loud and breathing soft,
Beseeching God, thy face to see.

CHARLES L. REASON

THE KING SENT AND RELEASED HIM,

THE RULER OF PEOPLES SET HIM FREE.

PSALM 105:20 NIV

I have often, in the deep stillness of a summer's Sabbath,
stood all alone upon the banks of that noble bay, and
traced, with saddened heart and tearful eye, the countless
number of sails moving off to the mighty ocean. The sight
of these always affected me powerfully. My thoughts would
compel utterance; and there, with no audience but the
Almighty, I would pour out my soul's complaint in my rude
way with an apostrophe to the moving multitude of ships.

—FREDERICK DOUGLASS

You are loosed from your moorings, and free. I am fast in my chains, and am a slave! You move merrily before the gentle gale, and I sadly before the bloody whip. You are freedom's swift-winged angels, that fly around the world; I am confined in bonds of iron.

O, that I were free! O, that I were on one of your gallant decks, and under your protecting wing! Alas! betwixt me and you the turbid waters roll. Go on, go on; O, that I could also go! Could I but swim! If I could fly! O, why was I born a man, of whom to make a brute! The glad ship is gone: she hides in the dim distance. I am left in the hell of unending slavery.

O, God, save me! God, deliver me! Let me be free!——Is there any God? Why am I a slave? I will run away. I will not stand it. Get caught or get clear, I'll try it. I had as well die with ague as with fever. I have only one life to lose. I had as well be killed running as die standing.

Only think of it: one hundred miles north, and I am free! Try it? Yes! God helping me, I will. It cannot be that I shall live and die a slave. I will take to the water. This very bay shall yet bear me into freedom.

The steamboats steer in a northeast course from North Point; I will do the same; and when I get to the head of the bay, I will turn my canoe adrift, and walk straight through Delaware into Pennsylvania. When I get there I shall not be required to have a pass: I will travel there without being disturbed. Let but the first opportunity offer, and come what will, I am off. Meanwhile I will try to bear the yoke.

I am not the only slave in the world. Why should I fret? I can bear as much as any of them. Besides I am but a boy yet, and all boys are bound out to someone. It may be that my misery in slavery will only increase my happiness when I get free. There is a better day coming.

Life and Times of Frederick Douglass, 1881

—⁓⁓—

EVENING PRAYER

*The present freedom and tranquility which you
enjoy you have mercifully received, and . . .
it is the peculiar blessing of Heaven.*

BENJAMIN BANNEKER

IF ANY OF YOU ARE SMART, YOU WILL LISTEN AND LEARN
THAT GOD ALL-POWERFUL DOES WHAT IS RIGHT.

JOB 34:10 CEV

Soul Cry

Father of Love!
We leave our souls with Thee!
Oh! may Thy Holy Spirit to us be
A peaceful Dove!

Now when day's strife
And bitterness are o'er,
Oh! in our hearts all bruised gently pour
The dew of life.

So as the rose—
Though fading on the stem—
Awakes to blush when morning's lustrous gem
Upon it glows;—

May we awake,
Soothed by Thy priceless balm,
To chant with grateful hearts our morning psalm,
And blessings take.

Or let it be,
That where the palm trees rise,
And crystal streams flow, we uplift our eyes
To Thee!—to Thee!

H. CORDELIA RAY

EVERY CROSS A CROWN OF JOY

Difficulty need not foreshadow despair or defeat.
Rather achievement can be all the more satisfying
because of obstacles surmounted.

WILLIAM HASTIE, *Grace Under Pressure*, 1984

IT WILL NO LONGER BE SAID TO YOU, "FORSAKEN," NOR TO
YOUR LAND WILL IT ANY LONGER BE SAID, "DESOLATE";
BUT YOU WILL BE CALLED, "MY DELIGHT IS IN HER,"
AND YOUR LAND, "MARRIED"; FOR THE LORD DELIGHTS
IN YOU, AND TO HIM YOUR LAND WILL BE MARRIED.

ISAIAH 62:4 NASB

By and by, when it was dark, Aunt Marthy came to see me.
She heard that Abram was sold, and she knew well enough how bad
I'd feel. Well, she sat down on the bed, and says, "Sally, I come to
pray with you, 'cause I know it's the only thing that'll do you any
good." I thought to myself, *There's no use in praying. Didn't I beg
the Lord to let my husband stay, and wasn't he sold all the same as*

if I hadn't asked Him? But I didn't speak, and so she knelt down and began.

At first I didn't pay any attention to what she said, but she kept on, and it appeared as like Lord Jesus was right in the room, and she was talking to Him. She told Him how afflicted I was, and how I was almost discouraged, and begged Him to stand by me, and to be better to me than the best husband in the world. All at once I thought perhaps this was the cross I had to carry for Jesus, and [it] appeared like a great burden rolled off my heart, and I could see my way clear through to heaven. Instead of grieving, I wanted to praise the Lord for His mercy. There was no trouble anymore; only the Lord; the Lord everywhere. When she was done praying I got up and began to sing this hymn. I'd often sung it before in the meetings, but I never knew what it meant until then:

> If there's a heavy cross to bear,
> Oh, Jesus! Master! show me where!
> And all for tender love of Thee,
> I'll bear it till it makes me free.
>
> Free from the faults I long have known;
> Free from the sins I dare not own;
> Free from each care the world has given,
> To keep my soul from Thee and heaven.

And when I reach that glorious place,

And gaze with rapture on Thy face,

Dear Jesus! every cross shall be

A crown of joy for Thee and me!

REV. ISAAC WILLIAMS

(Aunt Sally or the Cross, the Way of Freedom: A Narrative of the Slave-Life
and Purchase of the Mother of Rev. Isaac Williams of Detroit, Michigan)

—m—

I WILL BE WITH YOU

God has been profoundly real to me in recent years.
In the midst of outer dangers, I have felt an inner calm.
In the midst of lonely days and dreary nights I have
heard an inner voice saying, "Lo, I will be with you."

MARTIN LUTHER KING

HE LOOKED DOWN FROM HIS HOLY HEIGHT;
FROM HEAVEN THE LORD GAZED UPON THE EARTH.

PSALM 102:19 NASB

"He tied me with a rope by both arms and carried me to the smoke-house. When he got in he throwed the rope over the joist of the smoke-house and left me there all night. He just allowed my toes to touch the floor when he tied me up by my wrists. But, my child, the Lord was with me that night! I managed to get my wrists out of the rope, and I sat up nodding in the smoke-house all that night. I was afraid to let him see me down, so just as he was about to unlock the door the next day I slipped my hands back in the rope. He thought I had been tied all night; but, bless the Lord! I was just like Paul and Silas when they were in jail. I cried to the Lord, and He loosened the rope. Madam, although I did not have religion when I used to live in the woods, yet it seemed I could not keep from praying. I'd think of my mother, how, just before she died, she told me to 'come.' And that word always followed me. I used to lie out in the woods on the logs, with moss under my head, and pray a many and many a night. I hardly knowed what to say or how to pray, but I remembered how I used to hear my mother praying, on her knees, in the morning before day, long before she died, and I just tried to say what she used to say in her prayers. I heard her say many a time, 'O, Daniel's God, look down from heaven on me, a poor, needy soul!'

"I would say, 'O, Daniel's God, look down from heaven on me in these woods!'

"Sometimes it seemed I could see my mother right by my side as I laid on the log asleep. One time I talked with her in my sleep. I asked her, 'Mother, are you well?' And it seemed I could hear her saying, as she beckoned to me, 'Come, O come; will you come?' And I did try to get up in my sleep and start to her, and I rolled off the log. By that time I woke up, and the sun was shining clear and bright and I was there to wander about in the woods."

OCTAVIA V. ROGERS ALBERT,
The House of Bondage OR *Charlotte Brooks and Other Slaves*, 1890

—m—

O, DANIEL'S GOD!

We have lives in darker hours than those of today;
we have seen American justice and fair play go through
fire and death and devastation and come out purified
by the faith that abides in the God of Destiny.

ALEXANDER WALTERS

"I WILL HAVE MERCY ON WHOM I WILL HAVE MERCY,
AND I WILL HAVE COMPASSION ON
WHOM I WILL HAVE COMPASSION."

EXODUS 33:19 NIV

I told Warren about my dream of our mother, and that I saw her come up to me, and that I had been praying every night on my moss bed. I wanted to get him to pray too. I said to him, "Warren, you know how our poor mother used to pray way before day in the morning, and how we used to hear her cry. . . . And it makes me feel glad every time I pray, Warren; and now let us pray every time before we go to sleep."

Warren said, "Well, let us pray to Daniel's God just like our poor mother did." And we did every night before we went to sleep, after wandering all through the woods all day. Me and Warren would pray. We prayed low and easy; we just could hear each other. Warren used to pray, "O, Daniel's God, have mercy on me and Sallie. Mother said you will take care of us, but we suffer here; nobody to help us. Hear us way up in heaven and look down on us here."

We did not know hardly what to say, but we had heard mother and other people praying, and we tried to do the best we could. Sometimes we was so hungry we could hardly sleep, and it would be so cold, too, we did not know what to do. We had a big heap of moss, and we made a brush arbor over it to keep the rain off. I took Warren to the same place where I had been going at night in the chimney-corners to keep warm. But, la, madam, one morning we overslept ourselves and the overseer of that plantation caught us. He carried us home to old mistress. I heard her tell old master not to let the overseer hit us a lick. She said, "Send them to the kitchen and give them a plenty to eat and stop whipping them, and see if you can't do more with them." Madam, I tell you when I overheard her talking to master, tears came in my eyes. I told Warren. "O, how glad we felt that morning I cried for joy."

OCTAVIA V. ROGERS ALBERT,
The House of Bondage OR *Charlotte Brooks and Other Slaves*, 1890

—⚏—

IN THY CARE I KNOW NOT FEAR

We have come over a way that with tears
has been watered, We have come, reading our
path through the blood of the slaughtered.

JAMES WELDON JOHNSON

I WILL LIE DOWN IN PEACE AND SLEEP, FOR YOU ALONE,

O LORD, WILL KEEP ME SAFE.

PSALM 4:8 NLT

Soul Cry

LORD, within thy fold I be,
And I'm content;
Naught can be amiss to me,
For thy helping hand I see,
Light'ning loads that heavy be;
And I'm content.

Lord, I've put my trust in thee,
And I'm content.
Whatsoe'er my lot may be,
I have faith to rest in thee,
'Though my way I may not see;
And I'm content.

Lord, I feel thy Presence near,
And I'm content;
In thy care, I know not fear,
'Though the Tempter's voice I hear;
I'm secure when Thou art near;
And I'm content.

PRISCILLA JANE THOMPSON, 1900

HELP ME TO HELP MY CHILDREN

*Our children's allegiance to high goals
and standards will be principally established
and enforced, not on the campus, but in the home.*

HARRY EDWARDS

DON'T MAKE YOUR CHILDREN ANGRY BY THE WAY YOU
TREAT THEM. RATHER, BRING THEM UP WITH THE
DISCIPLINE AND INSTRUCTION APPROVED BY THE LORD.

EPHESIANS 6:4 NLT

Lord help me not to do for my children
what they can do for themselves.

Help me not to give them what they can earn for themselves.

Help me not to tell them what they can
look up and find out for themselves.

Help me to help my children stand on their own two feet
and to grow into responsible, disciplined adults.[8]

MARIAN WRIGHT EDELMAN,
Guide My Feet: Prayers and Meditations for Our Children

—⚏—

I SHALL PRAY!

*This very attempt to blot out forever the hopes of an enslaved
people may be one of the necessary links in the chain of events
preparatory to the complete overthrow of the whole slave system.*

FREDERICK DOUGLASS

IN MY DISTRESS I CRIED OUT TO THE LORD;
YES, I PRAYED TO MY GOD FOR HELP. HE HEARD ME
FROM HIS SANCTUARY; MY CRY REACHED HIS EARS.

PSALM 18:6 NLT

*Let others say what they will of the efficacy of prayer,
I believe in it, and I shall pray.*

—"ISABELLE" SOJOURNER TRUTH

"Oh, God, you know how much I am distressed, for I have told
you again and again. Now, God, help me get my son. If you were in
trouble, as I am, and I could help you, as you can me, think I
wouldn't do it? Yes, God, you know I would do it.

"Oh, God, you know I have no money, but you can make the people do for me, and you must make the people do for me. I will never give you peace till you do, God.

"Oh, God, make the people hear me—don't let them turn me off, without hearing and helping me."

And she has not a particle of doubt, that God heard her, and especially disposed the hearts of thoughtless clerks, eminent lawyers, and grave judges and others—between whom and herself there seemed to her almost an infinite remove—to listen to her suit with patient and respectful attention, backing it up with all needed aid.

[NARRATIVE OF SOJOURNER TRUTH, WRITTEN BY OLIVE GILBERT, BASED ON INFORMATION PROVIDED BY SOJOURNER TRUTH, 1850]

—⟪⟫—

I LEAVE THE REST TO YOU

No people that has solely depended on foreign aid or rather upon the efforts of those in any way identified with the oppressor to undo the heavy burdens, ever gained freedom.

FREDERICK DOUGLASS

Soul Cry

WE DEPEND ON THE LORD ALONE TO SAVE US.
ONLY HE CAN HELP US, PROTECTING US LIKE A SHIELD.
PSALM 33:20 NLT

Oh I Am who I Am

The God who protected and guided
Abraham, Isaac, Jacob and Moses

Who sent Joshua to fight the battle of Jericho,

Rescued Jonah from the belly of the whale
to take Your message to Ninevah,

Dispatched Ezra (whose name means "help") to proclaim
Your name and law and to revive Your people:

Protect and guide my beloved children by these
names to seek and to do Your will today.

Let them always feel Your faithful presence
wherever they go and in all their undertakings.

When they are confused, I pray they will wait for Your clarity.

When they are afraid, I pray they will seek Your soothing calm.

When they are alone, I pray they will feel
Your loving presence.

When they are sick, I pray You will lay
Your healing hand upon them.

When they are tired and overwrought, please lead them
to Your still waters of calm and restore their spirits.

When they face disappointments and dashed hopes and
friends and foe alike abandon them, let them find refuge
in Your never-changing faithfulness and love.

Oh I am who I am, I have done the best I know
how for my children. I leave the rest to You.[9]

MARIAN WRIGHT EDELMAN,
Guide My Feet: Prayers and Meditations for Our Children

—⁓—

I BELIEVE

In the beginning God . . . in the end God.
DESMOND TUTU

FEARING PEOPLE IS A DANGEROUS TRAP,
BUT TO TRUST THE LORD MEANS SAFETY.

PROVERBS 29:25 NLT

I believe, O God, that You are an eternal, incomprehensible spirit, infinite in all perfections, who did make all things out of nothing, and do govern them all by Your wise providence.

Let me always adore You with profound humility, as my Sovereign Lord; and help me to love and praise You with Godlike affections, and suitable devotion.

I believe that in the unity of the Godhead there is a trinity of persons, that You are perfectly one and perfectly three; one essence and three persons. I believe, O blessed Jesus, that You are of one substance with the Father, the very and eternal God, that You did take upon Yourself our frail nature, that You did truly suffer, and were crucified, dead and buried, to reconcile us to Your Father, and to be a sacrifice for sin.

I believe, that according to the types and prophecies which went before You, and according to Your own infallible prediction, You did by Your own power rise from the dead the third day, that You did ascend into Heaven, that there You sit on Your throne of glory adored by angels, and interceding for sinners.

I believe, that You have instituted and ordained holy mysteries as pledges of Your love, and for a continual commemoration of Your death; that You have not only given Yourself to die for me, but to be my spiritual food and sustenance in that holy sacrament, to my great and endless comfort. O may I frequently approach Your altar with humility and devotion, and work in me all those holy and heavenly affections, which become the remembrance of a crucified Savior.

I believe, O Lord, that You have not abandoned me to the dim light of my own reason, to conduct me to happiness; but that You have revealed in the holy Scriptures whatever is necessary for me to believe and practice, in order to ensure my eternal salvation.

O how noble and excellent are the precepts; how sublime and enlightening the truth; how persuasive and strong the motives; how powerful the assistances of Your holy religion, in which You have instructed me; my delight shall be in Your statutes, and I will not forget Your word.

I believe, it is my greatest honor and happiness to be Your disciple: how miserable and blind are those that live without God in the world, who despise the light of Your holy faith. Make me to part with all the enjoyments of life; nay, even life itself, rather than forfeit this jewel of great price. Blessed are the sufferings which are endured, happy is the death which is undergone for heavenly and immortal truth! I believe that You have prepared for those that love You, everlasting mansions of glory; if I believe You, O Eternal Happiness; why does anything appear difficult that leads to You? Why should I not willingly resist to the point of shedding my blood to obtain You? Why do the vain and empty employments of life take such fast hold of us? O perishing time! Why do You thus bewitch and deceive me? O Blessed Eternity! When shall You be my portion for ever?[10]

RICHARD ALLEN

BE BORN AGAIN IN OUR HEARTS

The experience of God, or in any case the possibility of experiencing God, is innate.

ALICE WALKER

"ALL THOSE WHO LOVE ME WILL DO WHAT I SAY.
MY FATHER WILL LOVE THEM, AND WE WILL
COME TO THEM AND LIVE WITH THEM."

JOHN 14:23 NLT

Jesus, small poor baby of Bethlehem,
Be born again in our hearts today,
Be born again in our homes today,
Be born again in our congregation today,
Be born again in our neighborhoods today,
Be born again in our cities today,
Be born again in our nations today,
Be born again in our world today.
Amen.[11]

MARIAN WRIGHT EDELMAN,
I'm Your Child, God: Prayers for Our Children

"I'll Never Let You Down"

I always felt a sense of cosmic companionship.
So that the loneliness and fear have faded away
because of a greater feeling of security.

MARTIN LUTHER KING JR.

"I'll never let you down, never walk off and leave you."

HEBREWS 13:5 MSG

He prayed for patience; Care and Sorrow came,
And dwelt with him, grim and unwelcome guests;
He felt their galling presence night and day;
And wondered if the Lord had heard him pray,
And why his life was filled with weariness.

He prayed again; and now he prayed for light;
The darkness parted, and the light shone in;
And lo! he saw the answer to his prayer—
His heart had learned, through weariness and care,
The patience, that he deemed he'd sought in vain.

CLARA ANN THOMPSON

WE SHALL OVERCOME

A child is a quicksilver fountain
spilling over with tomorrows and tomorrows
and that is why
she is richer than you and I.

TOM BRADLEY

LET US NOT NEGLECT OUR MEETING TOGETHER . . .
BUT ENCOURAGE AND WARN EACH OTHER, ESPECIALLY NOW
THAT THE DAY OF HIS COMING BACK AGAIN IS DRAWING NEAR.

HEBREWS 10:25 NLT

"We shall overcome" has got to be more than a frame of mind.
It's working hard in our own backyard—
to leave no children behind.
"We shall overcome" has got to be more than a children's prayer.
It's sacrifice, at any price, to show them that we care.
"We shall overcome" has got to be more than a memory.
It's a new resolve, to get involved in building a new community.
"We shall overcome" has got to be more than a distant dream.
And a place on the freedom team.

"We shall overcome" has got to be more than a protest song.

It's a loving vow, to show somehow, we all can get along.

"We shall overcome" has got to be more than a melody.

It's a one-by-one till the job is done to set the children free.

"We shall overcome" has got to be more than a freedom song.

It's confidence, being convinced that right will conquer wrong.

"We shall overcome" has got to be more than a song we sing.

It's a will to fight, to make things right, so the freedom bell can ring.

For the children ring,

For the children ring,

Through the power of the Spirit,

Let's empower each other

To go out with power

To set the children free.

To Set All the Children Free,

REV. JAMES FORBES, SENIOR MINISTER OF RIVERSIDE CHURCH, NEW YORK CITY

SILENCE IS MY DEEPEST CRY

Faith can give us courage to face
the uncertainties of the future.
MARTIN LUTHER KING JR.

I WAITED PATIENTLY FOR THE LORD TO HELP ME,
AND HE TURNED TO ME AND HEARD MY CRY.

PSALM 40:1 NLT

Out of the deep, I cry to Thee, oh Lord!
Out of the deep of darkness, and distress;
I cannot, will not doubt Thy blessed word,
Oh, God of righteousness!

I cry, and oh, my God, I know Thou'lt heed,
For Thou hast promised Thou wouldst
heed my cry;
I have no words to tell my deepest need,
Thou knowest oh, Most High!

Thou knowest all the pain,——the agony,
The grief I strive so vainly to express;

Soul Cry

Oh let Thy shelt'ring wings spread over me,

Great God of tenderness!

I cannot, cannot cease to cry to Thee,

For oh, my God, this heart is not my own,

And as the streams press ever to the sea,

My heart turns to Thy throne.

And when too weak to lift my voice, I lie

In utter silence at Thy blessed feet,

Thou'lt know, that silence is my deepest cry,

Thy throne, my last retreat.

And shouldst Thou hide Thy face for aye, from me,

My heart, though shattered, evermore would grope

Out through the darkness, still in search of Thee,

Oh God, my only hope!

CLARA ANN THOMPSON

SAVE ME!

Young man, Young Man,

Your arms are too short to box with God.

JAMES WELDON JOHNSON

"GO INTO ALL THE WORLD AND PREACH THE

GOOD NEWS TO EVERYONE, EVERYWHERE."

MARK 16:15 NLT

Lord, I want to go where You want me to go.

Do what You want me to do.

Be what You want me to be.

Save me!

—⟋⟍—

ON HIS MERCY LEAN

Lord, prop me up on my every leanin' side.

ANONYMOUS BLACK MINISTER

THEREFORE MY HEART IS GLAD AND MY TONGUE REJOICES;

MY BODY ALSO WILL REST SECURE.

PSALM 16:9 NIV

Is this the way, my Father,
That Thou would have me go—
Scaling the rugged mountain steep,
Or through the valley low?
Walking alone the path of life,
With timid, faltering feet;
Fighting with weak and failing heart,
Each conflict that I meet?

Nay! nay! my child, the Father saith,
Thou dost not walk alone—
Gird up the loins of thy weak faith,
And cease thy plaintive tone.
Look thou with unbeclouded eyes

Soul Cry

To Calvary's gory scene—
Canst thou forget the Savior's cries?
Go thou, on His mercy, lean.

My Father, brighter grows the way,
Less toilsome is the road;
If Thou Thy countenance display,
O, lighter seems my load!
And trustingly I struggle on,
Not murmuring o'er my task;
The mists that gather soon are gone,
When in Thy smile I bask.

Turn not from me Thy smiling face,
Lest I shall surely stray,
But in Thy loving arms' embrace,
I cannot lose my way.
My Father, when my faith is small,
And doubting fills my heart,
Thy tender mercy I recall.
O, let it ne'er depart!

JOSEPHINE HERD

Fix Me, Jesus!

Never let your head hang down. Never give up and
sit and grieve. Find another way. And don't pray
when it rains if you don't pray when the sun shines.

Satchel Paige

I command you—be strong and courageous!
Do not be afraid or discouraged.
For the LORD your God is with you wherever you go.

Joshua 1:9 nlt

Oh yes, fix me, Jesus, fix me.
Fix me so that I can walk on
a little while longer.
Fix me so that I can pray on
just a little bit harder.
Fix me so that I can sing on
just a little bit louder.
Fix me so that I can go on despite the pain,
The fear, the doubt, and yes, the anger.
I ask not that you take this cross from me,

only that you give me the strength to continue
carrying it onward 'til my dying day.
Oh, fix me, Jesus, fix me.

—◆—

TURN OUR HEARTS

Can't nobody but God handle your
whole heart without messing it up.

JEREMIAH WRIGHT

YOU HAVE BEEN CALLED FOR THIS PURPOSE, SINCE
CHRIST ALSO SUFFERED FOR YOU, LEAVING YOU
AN EXAMPLE FOR YOU TO FOLLOW IN HIS STEPS.

1 PETER 2:21 NASB

God of love,
turn our hearts to your ways;
and give us peace.
Amen.

PLEASE LISTEN

Man lives in God, and the circumference of life
cannot be rightly drawn until the center is set.

BENJAMIN MAYS

GOD KEEPS AN EYE ON HIS FRIENDS,
HIS EARS PICK UP EVERY MOAN AND GROAN.

PSALM 34:15 MSG

Lord in heaven,

please listen to all those

who are praying to You now.

Those who are sad and crying,

those who have lost friends and family.

Those who are alone

and frightened.

Help them to remember,

that You are there

and You are listening.

In Jesus' name, we pray. Amen.

—⁓⁓—

RESTORE ALL THINGS

Liberation is costly. It needs unity.
DESMOND TUTU

"I HAVE TOLD YOU ALL THIS SO THAT YOU MAY
HAVE PEACE IN ME. HERE ON EARTH YOU WILL
HAVE MANY TRIALS AND SORROWS. BUT TAKE HEART,
BECAUSE I HAVE OVERCOME THE WORLD."
JOHN 16:33 NLT

Almighty Father,
whose will is to restore all things
in Your beloved Son, the King of all:
govern the hearts and minds of those in authority,
and bring the families of the nations,
divided and torn apart by the ravages of sin,
to be subject to His just and gentle rule;
who is alive and reigns with You,
in the unity of the Holy Spirit,
one God, now and forever. Amen.

—◊◊◊—

SOMEBODY NEEDS YOU, GOD

The victory so courageously won in the street can easily
become an empty hollow mocker if we do not
simultaneously equip ourselves with the skills,
the values which the future will demand.

WHITNEY YOUNG

BY DAY THE LORD DIRECTS HIS LOVE, AT NIGHT HIS SONG
IS WITH ME—A PRAYER TO THE GOD OF MY LIFE.

PSALM 42:8 NIV

O God, our help in ages past, our hope for years to come—You are our shelter in the stormy blast, and our eternal home.

O God, my Father, I thank You tonight for Your loving kindness and Your tender mercies. Thank you, Holy Father, for Your blessed Word, a lamp for our feet and a light along our pathway. We want to thank You for Your Word that brought salvation. I want to thank You tonight, Lord God, that You included me a long time ago.

You shed Your blood on Calvary's cross, and gave Your life that I might live! I want to thank You tonight for it. You blest and enabled me to see You out of Your Word. I thank You for giving Your servant wisdom and power from his lips, for we have heard the gospel tonight.

O God, my Father, let Your Spirit ride, that the Word may find its place in the hearts of men and women, that it might bring forth fruit unto You. O God, let our coming not be in vain. Somebody needs You right now, O God, my Father. Would that You would convict and convert sinners that they might cry out, "What must I do to be saved?"

O God, let them not be satisfied until they've yielded their lives to be able to say, "I've fought a good fight. I have finished my course. I have kept the faith." I want to hear Your welcoming voice saying, "Enter into the joy of thy Master." Amen.

BANISH THE VIOLENCE

I've decided to stick with love.
Hate is too great a burden to bear.

MARTIN LUTHER KING JR.

WE KNOW HOW DEARLY GOD LOVES US,
BECAUSE HE HAS GIVEN US THE HOLY SPIRIT
TO FILL OUR HEARTS WITH HIS LOVE.

ROMANS 5:5 NLT

Lord,
remember Christ your Son who is peace itself
and who has washed away our hatred with His blood.
Because you love all people,
look with mercy on us.
Banish the violence and evil within us,
and in answer to our prayers restore tranquility and peace.
Amen.

I Stretch My Hand to You

Love has no awareness of merit or demerit; it has not scale by which its portions may be weighed or measured. It does not seek to balance giving and receiving. Love loves; this is its nature.

HOWARD THURMAN

YOUR BEAUTY AND LOVE CHASE AFTER ME
EVERY DAY OF MY LIFE. I'M BACK HOME IN
THE HOUSE OF GOD FOR THE REST OF MY LIFE.

PSALM 23:6 MSG

Father, I stretch my hand to You, for no other help I know. Oh, my rose of Sharon, my shelter in the time of storm. My prince of peace, my hope in this harsh land. We bow before You this morning to thank You for watching over us and taking care of us. This morning You touched us and brought us out of the land of slumber, gave us another day—thank You, Jesus.

We realize that many that talked as we now talk, this morning when their names were called, they failed to answer. Their voices were hushed up in death. Their souls had taken a flight and gone back to the God that gave it, but not so with us. We are thankful the sheet we covered with was not our winding sheet, and the bed we slept on was not our cooling board. You spared us and gave us one more chance to pray.

And, Father, before we go further, we want to pause and thank You for forgiving our sins. Forgive all our wrongdoings. We don't deserve it, but You lengthened out the prickly threads of our lives and gave us another chance to pray, and, Lord, for this we thank You. . . . Now, Lord, when I've come to the end of my journey, when praying days are done and time for me shall be no more; when these knees have bowed for the last time, when I too, like all others, must come in off the battlefield of life, when I'm through being 'buked and scorned, I pray for a home in glory.

When I come down to the river of Jordan, hold the river still and let your servant cross over during a calm down. Father, I'll be looking for that land where Job said the wicked would cease from troubling us and our weary souls would be at rest; over there where a thousand years is but a day in eternity, where I'll meet with loved ones and where I can sing praises to Thee; and we can say with the saints of old, Free at Last, Free at Last, thank God almighty, I am free at last. Your servant's prayer for Christ sake. Amen![12]

[TRADITIONAL PRAYER WITH ADDITIONS FROM REVEREND WALLACE EVANS]

THE RHYTHM THAT MAKES FOR LIFE

I believe in Patience—patience with the
weakness of the Weak and the strength of the Strong,
the prejudice of the Ignorant and the ignorance
of the Blind; patience with the tardy triumph of Joy
and the mad chastening of Sorrow; patience with God.

W. E. B. Du Bois

"BY STANDING FIRM, YOU WILL WIN YOUR SOULS."

LUKE 21:19 NLT

O God, slow us down and help us to see that we are put in charge of our lives, but with Thy help. Help us to get in tune with the rhythm that makes for life.

We keep moving, even though we know that we are made to center down, as well as to be actively engaged in the business of life. We compete for things and make those things more important than they ought to be. We eat what we ought not to eat. We neglect and misuse our bodies. We fail to discipline our minds and to be still and know that Thou art God and that we are the temple of the Most

High. Yet we often complain about our misfortunes and our hard luck, when at times it is we who are guilty of disregard.

Help us to know that we can be broken by life only if we first allow the victory of evil over our spirits.

May our hope and strength and faith be grounded in You; and may we recall the strength of our model, our brother and Your Son. Amen.

GEORGE THOMAS

—m—

NOT BY TERROR BUT IN LOVE

*Love is the force by which God binds man to himself
and man to man. Such love goes to the extreme;
it remains loving and forgiving even in the midst of hostility.*

JAMES LAWSON

"IF YOU ARE WILLING TO LISTEN, I SAY, LOVE YOUR ENEMIES.
DO GOOD TO THOSE WHO HATE YOU."

LUKE 6:27 NLT

Gracious God,

ruling the earth and its people

not by terror but in love,

we worship You.

We confess that too often

our words hurt others

and our deeds are selfish;

forgive us.

In this time of uncertainty and fear,

help us to love our enemies

and do good to those who hate us. Amen.

INFLAME MY HEART!

*Hatred paralyzes life; love releases it. Hatred confuses life;
love harmonizes it. Hatred darkens life; love illuminates it.*

MARTIN LUTHER KING JR.

THE ENTIRE LAW IS SUMMED UP IN A SINGLE COMMAND: "LOVE YOUR NEIGHBOR AS YOURSELF."

GALATIANS 5:14 NIV

O infinite amiableness! When shall I love You without bounds, without coldness or interruption which, alas! so often seize me here below? Let me never suffer any creature to be Your rival, or to share my heart with You; let me have no other God, no other love, but only You.

Whoever loves, desires to please the beloved object; and according to the degree of love is the greatness of desire; make me, O God, diligent and earnest in pleasing You; let me cheerfully discharge the most painful and costly duties; and forsake friends, riches, ease and life itself, rather than disobey You.

Whoever loves, desires the welfare and happiness of the beloved object; but You, O dear Jesus, can receive no addition from my imperfect services; what shall I do to express my affection towards You? I will relieve the necessities of my poor brethren, who are members of Your body; for he that loves not his brother whom he has seen, how can he love God whom he has not seen?

O crucified Jesus in whom I live, and without whom I die; mortify in me all sensual desires, inflame my heart with Your holy love, that I may no longer esteem the vanities of this world, but place my affections entirely on You.

Let my last breath, when my soul shall leave my body, breathe forth love to You, my God; I entered into life without acknowledging You, let me therefore finish it in loving You; O let the last act of life be love, remembering that God is love.[13]

RICHARD ALLEN,
The Life Experiences and Gospel Labors of the Rt. Rev. Richard Allen

I Will Hope in You

I'm here, I exist, and there's hope.

Vernon Jarrett

I will keep on hoping for you to help me;
I will praise you more and more.

Psalm 71:14 NLT

O, my God! In all my dangers temporal and spiritual I will hope in You who are Almighty power, and therefore able to relieve me; Who are infinite goodness, and therefore ready and willing to assist me.

O precious blood of my dear Redeemer! O gaping wounds of my crucified Saviour! Who can contemplate the sufferings of God incarnate, and not raise his hope, and not put his trust in Him. What though my body be crumbled into dust, and that dust blown over the face of the earth, yet I undoubtedly know my Redeemer lives, and shall raise me up at the last day; whether I am comforted or left desolate; whether I enjoy peace or am afflicted with temptations; whether I am healthful or sickly, succored or abandoned by the good things of this life, I will always hope in You, O my chiefest, infinite good.

Although the fig tree shall not blossom, neither shall fruit be in the vines; although the labor of the olive shall fail, and the fields yield no meat; although the flock shall be cut off from the fold, and there shall be no herd in the stalls, yet I will rejoice in the Lord, I will joy in the God of my salvation.

What though I mourn and am afflicted here, and sigh under the miseries of this world for a time, I am sure that my tears shall one day be turned into joy, and that joy none shall take from me. Whoever hopes for the great things in this world, takes pains to attain them; how can my hopes of everlasting life be well grounded, if I do not strive and labor for that eternal inheritance? I will never refuse the meanest labors, while I look to receive such glorious wages; I will never repine at any temporal loss, while I expect to gain such eternal rewards. Blessed hope! be my chief delight in life, and then I shall be steadfast and immoveable, always abounding in the work of the Lord; be my comfort and support at the hour of death, and then I shall contentedly leave this world, as a captive that is released from his imprisonment.[14]

RICHARD ALLEN,
The Life Experiences and Gospel Labors of the Rt. Rev. Richard Allen

—〰—

GOD OF ALL THE NATIONS

There are days when we can bring before God
a deep and glad laughter of joy and gratitude.
There will be other days when we can only muster a bitter,
angry complaint. If it is honest, be confident that God will
accept whatever it is we truly have to lift up before Him,
and He will make it serve His purpose and our good.

GARDNER TAYLOR

THEREFORE, SINCE WE HAVE BEEN MADE RIGHT IN GOD'S
SIGHT BY FAITH, WE HAVE PEACE WITH GOD BECAUSE
OF WHAT JESUS CHRIST OUR LORD HAS DONE FOR US.

ROMANS 5:1 NLT

Oh God of all the nations upon the earth! We thank You, that You are no respecter of persons, and that You have made of one blood all nations of men. We thank You, that You have appeared, in the fullness of time, in behalf of the nation from which most of the worshipping people, now before You, are descended. We thank You, that the Son of righteousness has at last shed His morning beams upon them.

Rend thy heavens, O Lord, and come down upon the earth; and grant that the mountains, which now obstruct the perfect day of Your goodness and mercy towards them, may flow down at Your presence. Send Your gospel, we beseech You, among them. May the nations, which now sit in darkness, behold and rejoice in its light. May Ethiopia soon stretch out her hands to You, and lay hold of the gracious promise of Your everlasting covenant.

Destroy, we beseech Thee, all the false religions, which now prevail among them; and grant that they may soon cast their idols to the moles and the bats of the wilderness. O, hasten that glorious time, when the knowledge of the gospel of Jesus Christ, shall cover the earth, as the waters cover the sea; when the wolf shall dwell with the lamb, and the leopard shall lie down with the kid, and the calf and the young lion falling together, and a little child shall lead them; and, when, instead of the thorn, shall come up the fir tree, and, instead of the brier, shall come up the myrtle tree: and it shall be to the Lord for a name and for an everlasting sign that shall not be cut off.

We pray, O God, for all our friends and benefactors in Great Britain, as well as in the United States: reward them, we beseech You, with blessings upon earth, and prepare them to enjoy the fruits of their kindness to us, in the everlasting kingdom in heaven; and dispose us, who are assembled in Thy presence, to be always thankful for Thy mercies, and to act as becomes a people who owe so much to Thy goodness. We implore Your blessing, O God, upon the President, and all who are in authority in the United States. Direct them by Your wisdom, in all their deliberations, and O save Your people from the calamities of war.

Give peace in our day, we beseech Thee, O thou God of peace! and grant that this highly favored country may continue to afford a safe and peaceful retreat from the calamities of war and slavery, for ages yet to come. We implore all these blessings and mercies, only in the name of Your beloved Son, Jesus Christ, our Lord.

And now, O Lord, we desire, with angels and archangels, and all the company of heaven, ever more to praise You, saying, "Holy, holy, holy, Lord God Almighty: the whole earth is full of Your glory." Amen.

ABSALOM JONES

TO WHOM SHALL I GO?

*Let not the shining thread of hope become so enmeshed
in the web of circumstance that we lose sight of it.*

CHARLES W. CHESTNUTT

AND NOW, LORD, WHAT WAIT I FOR? MY HOPE IS IN YOU.

PSALM 39:7 NKJV

O, Thou sin-forgiving God, they that are whole need not a
physician, but they that are sick. Lord, I am sick, and full of
diseases. If Thou wilt, Thou canst make me clean. Though my sins
have been as scarlet, Thou canst make them as wool; and though
they be red like crimson, Thou canst make them whiter than snow.

Were it not that there is a sufficiency in Thy blood to atone for
the vilest, the view of my past sins and transgression would sink me
in despair. But Thou hast said, him that cometh to Thee, Thou wilt
in no wise cast out.

Lord, I come, pleading alone the merits of my Redeemer; not
only for myself do I plead, but for the whole race of mankind;

especially for the benighted sons and daughters of Africa. Do Thou loose their bonds, and let the oppressed go free. Bless Thy churches throughout the world. Clothe Thy ministers with salvation, and cause Thy saints to shout for joy. Grant that the time may soon come, that all may know Thee from the rising of the sun unto the going down thereof.

MARIA W. STEWART, 1835

—⚉—

A HUMBLE, A BROKEN, A CONTRITE HEART

Lord, we ain't what we ought to be

And we ain't what we want to be.

We ain't what we gonna be, but thank God

We ain't what we were.

TRADITIONAL

Soul Cry

> COME, LET US BOW DOWN IN WORSHIP, LET US KNEEL BEFORE
> THE LORD OUR MAKER; FOR HE IS OUR GOD AND WE ARE
> THE PEOPLE OF HIS PASTURE, THE FLOCK UNDER HIS CARE.
>
> PSALM 95: 6-7 NIV

Our Father, who is in heaven, hallowed be Your name. Your kingdom come. Your will be done. Enable me to say from my heart, Your will be done, O God. The heaven is Your throne, and earth is Your footstool; neither may any say to You, what are You doing? But You are the high and lofty One who inhabits eternity, yet will You condescend to look upon him who is of a humble, a broken, and a contrite heart.

As such, enable me, O God, to bow before You at this time, under a deep sense of my guilt and unworthiness. It was my sins that caused You to arise in Your wrath against me. Be pleased, O God, to blot them from Your book, and remember them no more forever. Bless the church to which I belong. Your arm is not shortened that it cannot save, neither is Your ear heavy that it cannot hear; but it is our sins that have separated You from us. Purge us from all our dross; hide Your face from our iniquities, and speak peace to our troubled souls.

Bless Your servant, our pastor; let not this soul be discouraged, but may an angel appear to him, strengthening him. Bless all the benighted sons and daughters of Africa, especially my unconverted friends. Send them not away from Your presence into that large place that burns with fire and brimstone, but magnify the riches of Your grace in plucking their souls as brands from the burning; and though I may long sleep in death before You will perform this work, yet grant that in the resurrection morn we may all awake in Your likeness, and our souls be bound in the sure bundle of eternal life.[16]

MARIA W. STEWART

—◆—

GUIDE THE NATIONS

I was a drum major for justice.

MARTIN LUTHER KING JR.

WHEN HE, THE SPIRIT OF TRUTH
(THE TRUTH-GIVING SPIRIT) COMES,
HE WILL GUIDE YOU INTO ALL THE TRUTH
(THE WHOLE, FULL TRUTH).

JOHN 16:13 AMP

Almighty God, our heavenly Father,

guide the nations of the world into the way of justice and truth,

and establish among them that peace

which is the fruit of righteousness,

that they may become the kingdom of

our Lord and Savior Jesus Christ.

Amen.

—⚏—

NEW YEAR PRAYER

The past is a ghost, the future a dream. All we ever have is now.

BILL COSBY

MANY ARE SAYING OF ME, "GOD WILL NOT DELIVER HIM."

BUT YOU ARE A SHIELD AROUND ME, O LORD;

YOU BESTOW GLORY ON ME AND LIFT UP MY HEAD.

PSALM 3:2-3 NIV

Soul Cry

Our Father in Heaven, we come at this hour to express our sincere thanks for another year. We are thankful that You have spared these lives, and that You have brought them all the way through another year.

We pray that, as they conclude this old year and begin a new one, they will find joy, that they will find happiness, that they will find grace sufficient to take care of their needs. Our Father, we thank You for each one of them.

We thank You that they are still here, that they can still hear, that they are still able to feel, that they are still able to walk, and that they are still able to talk. We just want to thank You for these blessings as well as others.

Oh God, bless them. Bless their homes that they may continue to live in Your light. Bless each one here this morning, as well as those who were unable to come. Enable us to do the things that You would have us to do.

And, oh God, great God, we just thank You! We thank You Jesus! You have been so good to us! You have brought us such a long way. You lifted us up when we were down! You healed our sick bodies! You brought us a very long way. We want to thank You for it. You have fed us and kept us from being hungry. You have opened doors that were closed in our face. We want to thank You for it this morning.

And, oh God, we don't know whether we will be here another year or not! We can't depend on that. But we know that wherever we are, that where You are, everything will be all right! We want to thank You this morning, our Father. Take our hands and lead us on.

We ask in Your name. Amen.

WILLIAM TOWNSEND CRUTCHER, 1984

GRANT US A VISION

To demand freedom is to demand justice.
When there is no justice in the land, a man's
freedom is threatened. Freedom and justice are
interdependent. When a man has no protection under
the law it is difficult for him to make others recognize him.

JAMES CONE

I CAN DO EVERYTHING WITH THE HELP OF CHRIST

WHO GIVES ME THE STRENGTH I NEED.

PHILIPPIANS 4:13 NLT

Grant us, Lord God, a vision of our land

as Your love would make it:

A land where the weak are protected, and none go hungry or poor;

A land where the benefits of civilized life are shared,

and everyone can enjoy them;

A land where different races and cultures

live in tolerance and mutual respect;

A land where peace is built with justice,

and justice is guided by love.

And give us the inspiration and courage to build it,

through Jesus Christ our Lord.

Amen.

EULOGY FOR THE MARTYRED CHILDREN—MARTIN LUTHER KING JR., 1963

A SINGLE PEACE

Public peace is the act of public trust, it is the faith
that all are secure and will remain secure.

RICHARD WRIGHT

WHEN A MAN'S WAYS PLEASE THE LORD, HE MAKES

EVEN HIS ENEMIES TO BE AT PEACE WITH HIM.

PROVERBS 16:7 AMP

O God, who would fold both Heaven and earth in a single peace:

Let the design of Thy great love

lighten upon the waste of our wraths and sorrows:

and give peace to Your Church,

peace among nations,

peace in our dwellings,

and peace in our hearts:

through Your Son, our Savior Jesus Christ.

Amen.

Meet Me at the River, Lord

Preparation is hard work, running is the easy part.

Edwin Moses

"When everything is ready, I will come and get you,
so that you will always be with me where I am."

John 14:3 nlt

Almighty! and all wise God our heavenly Father! 'Tis once more and again that a few of your beloved children are gathered together to call upon Your holy name. We bow at Your footstool, Master, to thank You for our spared lives. We thank You that we were able to get up this morning clothed in our right mind. For, Master, since we met here, many have been snatched out of the land of the living and hurled into eternity.

But through Your goodness and mercy we have been spared to assemble ourselves here once more to call upon a captain who has never lost a battle. O throw round us Your strong arms of protection. Bind us together in love and union. Build us up where we are torn down and strengthen us where we are weak. O Lord! O Lord, take the lead of our minds, place them on heaven and heavenly divine things. O God, our captain and king! Search our hearts, and if You find anything there contrary to Your divine will just move it from us, Master, as far as the East is from the West.

Now, Lord, You know our hearts, You know our heart's desire. You know our down-setting and You know our up-rising. Lord, You know all about us because You made us. Lord! Lord! One more kind favor—I ask You to remember the man that is to stand in the gateway and proclaim Your Holy Word. O stand by him. Strengthen him where he is weak and build him up where he is torn down. O let him down into the deep treasures of Your Word.

And now, O Lord, when this humble servant is done down here in this low land of sorrow—done sitting down and getting up—done being called everything but a child of God—O when I am done, done, done, and this old world can afford me a home no longer, right soon in the morning, Lord, right soon in the morning—meet me down at the river of Jordan—bid the waters to be still—tuck my little soul away in the snow-white chariot and bear it away over yonder in the third heaven where every day will be a Sunday and my sorrows of this old world will have an end. This is my prayer for Christ my redeemer's sake. Let all say amen and thank God.[17]

REV. HAROLD A. CARTER

—◁◁◁—

PRAYER FOR PUBLIC LEADERS

My grandfather encouraged me by saying, "Why don't you do
what only you can do. Tell about the kids in the neighborhood.
Tell about things that happened to you when you were a child."

BILL COSBY

I URGE, THEN, FIRST OF ALL, THAT REQUESTS, PRAYERS,
INTERCESSION AND THANKSGIVING BE MADE FOR EVERYONE——
FOR KINGS AND ALL THOSE IN AUTHORITY.

1 TIMOTHY 2:1-2 NIV

O God our heavenly Father, whose love sets
no boundaries and whose strength is in service;
grant to the leaders of the nations wisdom, courage,
and insight at this time of darkness and fear.
Give to all who exercise authority determination to defend
the principles of freedom, love, and tolerance,
strength to protect and safeguard the innocent
and clarity of vision to guide the world into the paths of
justice and peace. This we ask through our Lord Jesus Christ.
Amen.

—⁓⁓—

NOW I LAY ME DOWN TO SLEEP

*Security is not an address. It's something you
carry with you wherever you go.*

ROZ RYAN

WHEN YOU LIE DOWN, YOU WILL NOT BE AFRAID;
WHEN YOU LIE DOWN, YOUR SLEEP WILL BE SWEET.

PROVERBS 3:24 NASB

Now I lay me down to sleep.
I pray the Lord my soul to keep.
If I should die before I wake,
I pray the Lord my soul to take.

"We Call Upon You"

*Faith can give us courage to face
the uncertainties of the future.*

MARTIN LUTHER KING JR.

WHATEVER YOU DO OR SAY, LET IT BE AS
A REPRESENTATIVE OF THE LORD JESUS, ALL THE WHILE
GIVING THANKS THROUGH HIM TO GOD THE FATHER.

COLOSSIANS 3:17 NLT

I thank Thee, Lord, for sparing me to see this morning, the blood running warm in my veins, the activity of my limbs and the use of my tongue. I thank You for raiment and for food, and above all, I thank You for the gift of Your darling Son Jesus, who came all the way from Heaven down to this low ground of sorrow, who died upon the Cross, that "whosoever believeth upon him should not perish but have everlasting life" (John 3:16 KJV).

Our Lord, our Heavenly Master, we ask You to teach us. Guide us in the way we know not. Give us more faith and a better understanding and a closer walk to Your bleeding side.

I have faith to believe You are the same God that was in the days that are past and gone. You heard Elijah praying in the cleft of the mountain. You heard Paul and Silas in jail. You heard the three Hebrew children in the fiery furnace. I have a faith to believe that You have once heard me pray, when I was laying and lugging around about the gates of hell, no eye to pity me, no arm to save me. You reached down Your long arm of protection and snatched my soul from the midst of eternal burning. You placed me in the rock and placed a new song in my mouth. You told me to go, and You would go with me; open my mouth, and You would speak for me.

For that cause we call upon You at this hour. And while we call upon You, we ask You, please don't go back on Glory, neither turn a deaf ear to our call. But turn down the kindness of a listening ear, catch our moans and groans, and take them home to the High Heavens. We plead boldly one thing more, if 'tis Your glorious will, I pray.

O Lord, our Heavenly Master, we ask You please to search our hearts. Tie the reins of our minds. If You see anything laying and lugging around our hearts, not Your right hand planted and neither pleasing to Your sight, we ask You to remove it by the brightness of Your coming, cast it in the sea of forgiveness, where it will never rise up against us in this world, neither condemn us at the bar of judgment, if it is Your glorious will, I pray.

O God, our Heavenly Father, we ask You to please make us a better servant in the future than we have been in the past, and may our last days be our best days.

We thank You, our Heavenly Father, for what You have done for us in days that are past and gone, and what You are doing at this present moment. I know You have been good to me, because You have brought me a mighty long ways. Through many dangers, toils, and snares I have already come. 'Twas grace that brought me safe thus far, and grace will lead me on.

O Lord, our Heavenly Father, will You please have mercy; please remember the sick and the afflicted, the poor and those in hospitals, bodies racked in pain, scorched with parching fever; have mercy on them if 'tis Your glorious will, I pray.

O Lord, my Heavenly Master, remember this weak and unprofitable servant made the attempt to bow before You. Go behind me as a protecting angel, and by my side as a safeguard. And when we have done all assigned to our hands to do, this old world can afford us a home no longer, may we look back and see a well-spent life and just before a joyful hour, that we may be able to sing praise to the Father, Son, One God, world without end. My soul say amen, amen, amen.[18]

REV. HAROLD A. CARTER

"WE CAN STAND TALL"

Hold fast to Faith. Desert not the ranks, but as brave soldiers march on to victory. I am happy and shall remain so as long as you keep the flag flying.

MARCUS GARVEY

LOOK AT THE PROUD! THEY TRUST IN THEMSELVES,
AND THEIR LIVES ARE CROOKED;
BUT THE RIGHTEOUS WILL LIVE BY THEIR FAITH.

HABAKKUK 2:4 NLT

As men of God, Creator and Maker of All,
we are determined to STAND!
We are Strong and Weak,
Rich and Poor;

Do not define us by what we do
and who we know;
We belong to God.

We love the Lord and our families,
We plant and build and play.

We are STRONG.
Even when we hurt so bad that
if we cried out in pain,

All creation would groan;
The earth would tremble and shake.
We hold our pain in
and pretend it's not there.

Don't let our masks make you think
we don't care;
We care, we care deeply.
We're proud of our fathers, natural and adopted,
We honor and respect our mothers at home and afar,
Our sisters and brothers are closer than many,
Our friends share our growing pains
and make us laugh.
Our wives and partners share a bond with us,
and intimacy with us and God.
Our children are our seed, the essence of our love.
We are ourselves, noble and free,
Bold warriors, gentle guides,
Searching for our destiny.

We remember our history.
We inherit the evils of slavery and racism.
We remember the time we've been

Soul Cry

"buked and scorned,"

The times our parents were humiliated.

We remember that Jesus truly loves us.

We know that as men, we can STAND TALL,

Love,

Organize,

Create,

Be Somebody,

Do Good.

We are already somebody!

With God's grace we can save

our churches,

our communities,

Our boys,

Our girls,

OURSELVES.

THE 1998 NATIONAL BLACK MEN'S CONFERENCE, ATLANTA, GEORGIA

—◊◊◊—

TO BELIEVE IN OURSELVES

If you don't have confidence,
you'll always find a way not to win.

CARL LEWIS

WE CAN BE CONFIDENT THAT HE WILL LISTEN TO US WHENEVER
WE ASK HIM FOR ANYTHING IN LINE WITH HIS WILL.

I JOHN 5:14 NLT

Now, great God, give us Thy power to believe in ourselves,
and in what we can do, and in what we can be, and in what we are.
May the grace of Jesus Christ be with us all. Amen.

—⚬—

THE GLORIOUS HOPE

Out of the sighs of one generation are kneaded the hopes
of the next.

JOAQUIM MACHADO DE ASSIS

GOD'S EYE IS ON THOSE WHO RESPECT HIM,

THE ONES WHO ARE LOOKING FOR HIS LOVE.

HE'S READY TO COME TO THEIR RESCUE

IN BAD TIMES; IN LEAN TIMES

HE KEEPS BODY AND SOUL TOGETHER.

PSALM 33:18-19 MSG

Almighty God, it is the glorious hope of a blessed immortality beyond the grave that supports Your children through this vale of tears. Forever blessed be Your name, that You have implanted this hope in my bosom.

If You have indeed plucked my soul as a brand from the burning, it is not because You have seen any worth in me; but it is because of Your distinguishing mercy, for mercy is Your darling attribute, and You delight in mercy, and are not willing that any should perish, but that all should come to the knowledge of the truth as it is in Jesus.

Clothe my soul with humility as with a garment. Grant that I may bring forth the fruits of a meek and quiet spirit. Enable me to adorn the doctrines of God my Savior, by a well regulated life and conversation. May I become holy, even as You are holy, and pure, even as You are pure.

Bless all my friends and benefactors: those who have given me a cup of cold water in Your name, the Lord reward them. Forgive all my enemies. May I love those who hate me, and pray for those who despitefully use and persecute me. Preserve me from slanderous tongues, O God, and let not my good be spoken evil of. Let not a repining thought enter my heart, nor a murmuring sigh heave from my bosom. But may I cheerfully bear with all the trials of life.

Clothe me with the pure robes of Christ's righteousness, that when He shall come in flaming fire to judge the world, I may appear before Him with joy. Not only for myself do I ask these blessings, but for all the sons and daughters of Adam, as You are no respecter of persons, and as all distinctions wither in the grave.

Grant all prejudices and animosities may cease from among men. May we all realize that promotion comes not from the East nor from the West, but that it is God who puts up one and sets down another. May the rich be rich in faith and good words towards our

Lord Jesus Christ, and may the poor have an inheritance among the saints in light, a crown incorruptible that fades not away, eternal in the heavens.

And now what do we wait for? Be pleased to grant that we may at last join with all the Israel of God, in celebrating Your praises.[19]

MARIA W. STEWART, 1835

—◇—

"ON THIS THANKSGIVING DAY"

God gives nothing to those who keep their arms crossed.

AFRICAN PROVERB

HONOR THE LORD WITH YOUR WEALTH AND WITH THE
BEST PART OF EVERYTHING YOUR LAND PRODUCES.
THEN HE WILL FILL YOUR BARNS WITH GRAIN, AND
YOUR VATS WILL OVERFLOW WITH THE FINEST WINE.

PROVERBS 3:9-10 NLT

Dear Lord, we thank Thee for the crops
Of white and golden grain,
Which now are safely gathered in
From winter's sleet and rain!

And for the fruits and for the foods
In cellars stored away;
We thank Thee now, dear blessed Lord,
On this Thanksgiving Day!

Not only for the crops this year
(So bounteous and free)
Of grain and fruit so plenteous
Do we give thanks to Thee;

But for the many gifts which Thou
Hast on us all bestowed;
Each day, each hour and all the time,
We thank Thee, blessed Lord!

EFFIE WALLER SMITH

A MIGHTY SHAKING OF DRY BONES

*My hope for my children must be that they respond
to the still, small voice of God in their own hearts.*

ANDREW YOUNG

BECAUSE OF THE LORD'S GREAT LOVE WE ARE NOT
CONSUMED, FOR HIS COMPASSIONS NEVER FAIL.
THEY ARE NEW EVERY MORNING.

LAMENTATIONS 3:22-23 NIV

O, Lord God, the watchmen of Zion have cried peace, when there was no peace; they have been, as it were, blind leaders of the blind. Wherefore have You so long withheld from us the divine influences of Your Holy Spirit? Wherefore have You hardened our hearts and blinded our eyes? It is because we have honored You with our lips, when our hearts were far from You. We have regarded iniquity in our hearts, therefore You will not hear.

Return again to us. O Lord God, we beseech You, and pardon this the iniquity of Your servants. Cause Your face to shine upon us, and we shall be saved. O visit us with Your salvation. Raise up sons and daughters of Abraham, and grant that there might come a

~111~

mighty shaking of dry bones among us, and a great ingathering of souls. Quicken Your professing children. Grant that the young may be constrained to believe that there is a reality in religion and a beauty in the fear of the Lord. Have mercy on the blighted sons and daughters of Africa. Grant that we may soon become so distinguished for our moral and religious improvements, that the nations of the earth may take knowledge of us; and grant that our cries may come up before Your throne like holy incense.

Grant that every daughter of Africa may consecrate her sons to Thee from the birth. And, Lord, do bestow upon them wise and understanding hearts. Clothe us with humility of souls, and give us a becoming dignity of manners: may we imitate the character of the meek and lowly Jesus; and do grant that Ethiopia may soon stretch forth her hands unto You.

And now, Lord, be pleased to grant that Satan's kingdom may be destroyed; that the kingdom of our Lord Jesus Christ may be built up; that all nations, and hundreds, and tongues, and people might be brought to the knowledge of the truth, as it is in Jesus, and we at last meet around Thy throne, and join in celebrating Thy praises.

MARIA W. STEWART, 1835

—m—

"But for Thy Grace Lost Would I Be"

God of our weary years,
God of our silent tears,
Thou who hast brought us this far on the way;
Thou who hast by Thy might
Let us into the light,
Keep us forever in the path, we pray.

James Weldon Johnson

The people all tried to touch him, because power
was coming from him and healing them all.

Luke 6:19 niv

O God, to Thee I come today,
And with true repentance kneeling,
The while I bend my knee to pray,
The tears from mine eyes are stealing.

But for Thy grace lost would I be,
Or ship-wrecked on life's hidden shoals,
Or left to drift upon the sea,
Where dwelleth all earth's derelict souls.

But Thou didst free from all alarms
And shield me from the tempter's power;
Thou broke the shackles from my arms,
And Thou didst cheer my darkest hour.

Thou hast supplied my every need,
And made me free, and free indeed.

THEODORE HENRY SHACKELFORD

"GROAN THE WORDS I FAIN WOULD SPEAK"

Man is a peculiar creature—he is the image of his God, though he may be subject to the most wretched conditions upon earth, yet the spirit and feeling which constitute the creature, man, can never be entirely erased from his breast, because the God who made him after his own image, planted it in his heart.

DAVID WALKER

Soul Cry

THE MOMENT WE GET TIRED IN THE WAITING, GOD'S SPIRIT
IS RIGHT ALONGSIDE HELPING US ALONG. IF WE DON'T
KNOW HOW OR WHAT TO PRAY, IT DOESN'T MATTER.
HE DOES OUR PRAYING IN AND FOR US, MAKING PRAYER
OUT OF OUR WORDLESS SIGHS, OUR ACHING GROANS.

ROMANS 8:26 MSG

My God, sometimes I cannot pray,
Nor can I tell why thus I weep;
The words my heart has framed I cannot say,
Behold me prostrate at Thy feet.

Thou understandest all my woe;
Thou knows't the craving of my soul—
Thine eye beholdeth whereso'er I go;
Thou can'st this wounded heart make whole.

And oh! while prostrate here I lie,
And groan the words I fain would speak:
Unworthy though I be, pass not me by,
But let Thy love in showers break.

And deluge all my thirsty soul,
And lay my proud ambition low;

So while time's billows o'er me roll,
I shall be washed as white as snow.

Thou wilt not quench the smoking flax,
Nor wilt Thou break the bruised reed;
Like potter's clay, or molten wax,
Mould me to suit Thy will indeed.[20]

JOSEPHINE HENDERSON HERD

—⁕—

"KEEP ME IN THY CARE"

*There will always be men struggling to change, and there
will always be those who are controlled by the past.*

ERNEST J. GAINES

HE WILL FEED HIS FLOCK LIKE A SHEPHERD.
HE WILL CARRY THE LAMBS IN HIS ARMS,
HOLDING THEM CLOSE TO HIS HEART.
HE WILL GENTLY LEAD THE MOTHER SHEEP WITH THEIR YOUNG.

ISAIAH 40:11 NLT

Soul Cry

Oh, Lord! I lift my heart,
In gratitude, to Thee,
For blessings, manifold,
Thou hast bestowed on me.

When conflicts raged within,
Too blinding to express,
Thou pitied my still tongue,
And soothed my heart to rest.

Keep me within Thy care;
Compel me, to the right;
'Tis sweet to walk with Thee,
In darkness or in light.

PRISCILLA JANE THOMPSON, *Gleanings of Quiet Hours*

"MY SPIRIT STRIVES FOR THEE"

There isn't a certain time we should set aside to talk about God.
God is part of our every waking moment.

MARVA COLLINS

I PLEAD WITH YOU TO GIVE YOUR BODIES TO GOD.
LET THEM BE A LIVING AND HOLY SACRIFICE—
THE KIND HE WILL ACCEPT. WHEN YOU THINK OF WHAT
HE HAS DONE FOR YOU, IS THIS TOO MUCH TO ASK?

ROMANS 12:1 NLT

Oh God! my heart is Thine,
Content, am I in Thee;
Thy chast'ning rod but proves,
That Thou, abide with me.

I know Thou leadeth on,
But oh, the way is drear;
Naught, but the click of thorns,
Is sounding in my ear.

I cry, "Thy will be done!"
My heart is with the cry;

Soul Cry

Yet comes not light, nor peace,
To soothe my tear-dim eye.

My heart craves earthly things;
I feel its nature's claim;
Since Thou didst give me life,
Canst I discard an aim?

The hot blood stirs my brain,
And sweet dreams to me flock:
Alas! I see them wrecked,
Upon Ambition's rock.

Oh Christ! Come down to earth,
An elder brother, be;
And pilot Thou, my barque,
Which drifts, capriciously.

Oh wrench me from the toils,
Of this entangled mesh!
My spirit strives for Thee,
Despite the erring flesh.

PRISCILLA JANE THOMPSON, *Gleanings of Quiet Hours*

"MY HEART IS HEAVY LADEN

We've moved God out of the stained-glass prison that
so many religious leaders have locked him into.

MARVIN WINANS

GIVE ALL YOUR WORRIES AND CARES TO GOD,
FOR HE CARES ABOUT WHAT HAPPENS TO YOU.

1 PETER 5:7 NLT

O, Father, my heart is heavy laden,
And grief has settled over me like pall;
And behold in earth and Heaven,
My anguished soul on none but thee can call.

No one but thee a word of cheer can give,
In this the deepened gloom of a sad day;
Oh, come to my heart, dear Father,
And bid my bitter sorrow steal away.

Teach me to see how blessed good shall come
From everything that seemeth to me ill;
If I but wait, but trust my all to thee
And ever seek to do thy loving will.

Soul Cry

And while I cannot see a ray of light,
Yet lend me faith to love thee well;
And conquering grace for every trial,
Till I beyond the pearly gates shall dwell.

Tonight I need thy rod and staff
To comfort me, for I am travel-worn;
My hands are weary with much toil,
My feet are badly bruised and torn.

Reach down and hide me in thy cleft,
Where I may rest awhile my weary feet;
And there I pray that thine own voice
In soothing tones my longing heart shall greet.

So shall I then be comforted,
My soul shall then rejoice in thee;
The oil of joy thy presence sheds
Shall fill my soul with ecstacy.

KATHERINE DAVIS CHAPMAN TILLMAN, 1896

"A RECORD OF THE DAY"

To be successful, grow to the point where one completely
forgets himself; that is, to lose himself in a great cause.

BOOKER T. WASHINGTON

I HAVE FOUGHT A GOOD FIGHT, I HAVE FINISHED
THE RACE, AND I HAVE REMAINED FAITHFUL.

2 TIMOTHY 4:7 NLT

Oh Lord, the work Thou gavest me
With this day's rising sun,
Through faith and earnest trust in Thee,
My Master, it is done.

And ere I lay me down to rest,
To sleep—perchance for aye—
I'd bring to Thee at Thy request
A record of the day.

And while I bring it willingly
And lay it at Thy feet,

I know, oh, Savior, certainly,
  That it is not complete.

Unless Thy power and grace divine,
  Upon what I have wrought,
Shall in its glorious fulness shine,
  Oh Lord, the work is naught.

BY LUCY HUGHES BROWN, M.D.

—Taken from *The Work of the Afro-American Woman*, Mrs. N. F. Mossell, 1908

—∽∾—

"MY SOUL WOULD FLY AWAY"

*We have to do with the past only as we can
make it useful to the present and to the future.*

FREDERICK DOUGLASS

NO, DEAR BROTHERS AND SISTERS, I AM STILL NOT
ALL I SHOULD BE, BUT I AM FOCUSING ALL
MY ENERGIES ON THIS ONE THING: FORGETTING THE
PAST AND LOOKING FORWARD TO WHAT LIES AHEAD.

PHILIPPIANS 3:13 NLT

Soul Cry

Oh God, my soul would fly away
Were it not fettered by this clay;
I long to be with Thee at rest,
To lean in love upon Thy breast.

Here in this howling wilderness,
With enemies to curse, not bless,
I feel the need of Thy strong hand
To guide me to that better land.

How oft, oh God, I feel the sting
Of those whose evil tongues would wring
The heart of any trusting one
As did the Jews to Thy dear Son.

Yet in this hour of grief and pain,
Let me not curse and rail again;
But meek in prayer, Lord, let me go
And say, "They know not what they do."

Lord, when this hard-fought battle's o'er,
And I shall feel these stings no more,
Then let this blood-washed spirit sing
Hosannah to my Lord and King.

BY LUCY HUGHES BROWN, M.D.

—Taken from *The Work of the Afro-American Woman*, Mrs. N. F. Mossell, 1908

SAVE YOUR SOUL

Hate sin; love God; religion be your prize;
Here laws obeyed will surely make you wise,
Secure you from the ruin of the vain,
And save your souls from everlasting pain.

DANIEL PAYNE

"IS NOT THIS MAN A BURNING STICK SNATCHED FROM THE FIRE?"

ZECHARIAH 3:2 NIV

I was converted when fifteen years old. It was on a Sunday evening at a quarterly meeting. The minister preached from the text: "And they sung as it were a new song before the throne, and before the four beasts, and the elders: and no man could learn that song but the hundred and forty and four thousand, which were redeemed from the earth" (Revelation 14:3).

As the minister dwelt with great force and power on the first clause of the text, I beheld my lost condition as I never had done before. Something within me kept saying, *Such a sinner as you are can never sing that new song.*

~125~

No tongue can tell the agony I suffered. I fell to the floor, unconscious, and was carried home. Several remained with me all night, singing and praying. I did not recognize anyone, but seemed to be walking in the dark, followed by someone who kept saying, "Such a sinner as you are can never sing that new song." Every converted man and woman can imagine what my feelings were. I thought God was driving me on to hell.

In great terror I cried: *"Lord, have mercy on me, a poor sinner!"*

The voice which had been crying in my ears ceased at once, and a ray of light flashed across my eyes, accompanied by a sound of far distant singing; the light grew brighter and brighter, and the singing more distinct, and soon I caught the words: "This is the new song—redeemed, redeemed!" I at once sprang from the bed where I had been lying for twenty hours, without meat or drink, and commenced! singing: "Redeemed! redeemed! glory! glory!" Such joy and peace as filled my heart, when I felt that I was redeemed and could sing the new song. Thus was I wonderfully saved from eternal burning.

(*A Brand Plucked from the Fire: An Autobiographical Sketch*,
MRS. JULIA A. J. FOOTE, 1886)

ENDURE TO THE END

Keep on moving, keep on insisting,
keep on fighting injustice.

MARY CHURCH TERRELL

YOU KNOW HOW WE CALL THOSE BLESSED (HAPPY)
WHO WERE STEADFAST [WHO ENDURED].

JAMES 5:11 AMP

In the midst of life and deeds it is easy to have endurance and strength and determination, but Thy Word, O Lord, teaches us that this is not enough to bring good to the world—to bring happiness and the worthier success. For *this* we must endure to the end, learn to finish things, to bring them to accomplishment and full fruition. We must not be content with plans, ambitions, resolves; with part of the message or part of an education, but be set and determined to fulfill the promise and complete the task and secure the full training. Such men and women alone does God save by lifting them above and raising them to higher worlds and wider prospects. Give us, O God, to resist today the temptation of shirking, and the grit to endure to the end. Amen.

W. E. B. DU BOIS

An Unwavering Faith

Of all the needs (there are none imaginary)
a lonely child has, the one that must be satisfied,
if there is going to be hope and a hope of wholeness,
is the unshaken need for an unshakable God.

Maya Angelou

I lift up my eyes to the hills—
where does my help come from? My help comes
from the LORD, the Maker of heaven and earth.

Psalm 121:1-2 NIV

"My children, there is a God, who hears and sees you."

"A God, mau-mau! Where does He live?" asked the children.

"He lives in the sky," she replied, "and when you are beaten, or cruelly treated, or fall into any trouble, you must ask help of Him, and He will always hear and help you."

She taught them to kneel and say the Lord's Prayer. She entreated them to refrain from lying and stealing, and to strive to obey their masters. At times, a groan would escape her, and she would break out in the language of the Psalmist,

"Oh Lord, how long? Oh Lord, how long?"

And in reply to Isabella's question—"What ails you, mau-mau?" her only answer was, "Oh, a good deal ails me—Enough ails me." Then again, she would point them to the stars, and say, in her peculiar language, "Those are the same stars, and that is the same moon, that look down upon your brothers and sisters, and which they see as they look up to them, though they are ever so far away from us, and each other."

Thus, in her humble way, did she endeavor to show them their Heavenly Father, as the only being who could protect them in their perilous condition; at the same time, she would strengthen and brighten the chain of family affection, which she trusted extended itself sufficiently to connect the widely scattered members of her precious flock. These instructions of the mother were treasured up and held sacred by Isabella, as our future narrative will show.

In these hours of her extremity, she did not forget the instructions of her mother, to go to God in all her trials, and every affliction; and she not only remembered, but obeyed: going to Him, "and telling Him all—and asking Him if He thought it was right," and begging Him to protect and shield her from her persecutors.

She always asked with an unwavering faith that she should receive just what she plead for.

"And now," she say, "though it seems curious, I do not remember ever asking for anything but what I got it. And I always received it as an answer to my prayers."

Narrative of Sojourner Truth, WRITTEN BY OLIVE GILBERT, BASED ON INFORMATION PROVIDED BY SOJOURNER TRUTH, 1850

—ɱ—

NO EASY WALK

There is no easy walk to freedom anywhere, and many of us will have to pass through the valley of the shadow of death again and again before we reach the mountaintop of our desires.

NELSON MANDELA

EVERYTHING THAT WAS WRITTEN IN THE PAST WAS WRITTEN TO TEACH US, SO THAT THROUGH ENDURANCE AND THE ENCOURAGEMENT OF THE SCRIPTURES WE MIGHT HAVE HOPE.

ROMANS 15:4 NIV

Soul Cry

Lead gently, Lord, and slow,
For, oh, my steps are weak,
And ever as I go,
Some soothing sentence speak;
That I may turn my face
Through doubt's obscurity
Toward thine abiding-place,
Even though I cannot see.

For lo, the way is dark;
Through mist and cloud I grope,
Save for that fitful spark,
The little flame of hope.

Lead gently, Lord, and slow,
For fear that I may fall;
I know not where to go
Unless I hear Thy call.

My fainting soul doth yearn
For Thy green hills afar;
So let Thy mercy burn—
My greater, guiding star!

PAUL LAWRENCE DUNBAR

I'll Follow Thee

Precious Lord, take my hand, Lead me on, let me stand.
I am tired, I am weak, I am worn.
Through the storm, through the night, lead me on to the light.

TOMMY DORSEY

THIS SUFFERING IS ALL PART OF WHAT GOD HAS
CALLED YOU TO. CHRIST, WHO SUFFERED FOR YOU,
IS YOUR EXAMPLE. FOLLOW IN HIS STEPS.

1 PETER 2:21 NLT

My Savior, let me hear Thy voice tonight,
I'll follow Thee, I'll follow Thee;
The clouds that overhang my way, obscure the light,
And all is dark to me.

I'd hear Thy voice above the tempest's shriek;
I'll follow Thee, I'll follow Thee;
And though my sight be dim, my spirit weak,
I'll trust, though naught I see.

I'd feel Thy arm, supporting in the dark;
I'll follow Thee, I'll follow Thee;
For Thou canst fan to flame, faith's sinking spark,
And seal my loyalty.

I shall not sink, dear Lord, when Thou'rt my guide,
I'll follow Thee, I'll follow Thee;
Though lashed by heavy waves, on ev'ry side,
I'm safe, when Thou'rt with me.

CLARA ANN THOMPSON

—∿—

ALL I AM AND HOPE TO BE

Our creator is the same and never changes despite the names
given Him by people here and in all parts of the world.
Even if we gave Him no name at all, He would still be there,
within us, waiting to give us good on this earth.

GEORGE WASHINGTON CARVER

TAKE YOUR EVERYDAY, ORDINARY LIFE——YOUR SLEEPING,
EATING, GOING-TO-WORK, AND WALKING-AROUND LIFE——
AND PLACE IT BEFORE GOD AS AN OFFERING. EMBRACING WHAT
GOD DOES FOR YOU IS THE BEST THING YOU CAN DO FOR HIM.

ROMANS 12:1 MSG

Lord, all I am and hope to be,

I humbly offer, King, to thee!

When clouds arise, thy guidance send,

Accept my life, and bless it, Friend.

O Father! let me rest in thee,

Resigned to what *thou* will'st for me;

Content, though all my fond hopes fade,

And visions bright in gloom are laid.

When I was but a tiny child,

Thou shielded me from tempests wild;

And gave me strength to do the right

Within temptation's treacherous sight.

And now in girlhood's solemn time,

Oh, make my life one perfect rhyme,

Sung to the air of sweet content,

With blended sounds of a life well spent.[21]

ELOISE ALBERTA VERONICA BIBB, *Poems by Eloise Bibb*, 1895.

LET ME DIE FIGHTING

There will be no way to avoid a degree of suffering, of trial, or tribulation; suffering comes to all people, but you have within your power the means to make the suffering of your people meaningful to redeem whatever stresses and strains may come.

RICHARD WRIGHT

ENDURE SUFFERING ALONG WITH ME, AS A GOOD SOLDIER OF CHRIST JESUS. AND AS CHRIST'S SOLDIER, DO NOT LET YOURSELF BECOME TIED UP IN THE AFFAIRS OF THIS LIFE, FOR THEN YOU CANNOT SATISFY THE ONE WHO HAS ENLISTED YOU IN HIS ARMY.

2 TIMOTHY 2:3-4 NLT

John was ready mentally, physically and spiritually. The night before when he realized that the zero hour was at hand he walked out of his barracks into the darkness. As he walked he sang softly the old Negro spiritual, "Walk with me Lord, walk with me while I'm on dis Pilgrim jou'ney, Lord, I want Jesus to walk with me."

He knelt by his cot in the darkness of the barracks and offered a fervent prayer for strength to be a good and brave soldier and to return alive. John had prayed further,

"If I must die, Lord, let me die fighting with all my heart and soul and the last breath that is within me for the freedom of my family and race."[22]

I Wouldn't Take Nothing for My Journey, LEONIDAS H. BERRY, M.D.

—⁂—

GUIDE AND PROTECT

Let us gather around our children and give them the security that can only come from association with adults who mean what they say and share in deeds which are broadcast in words.

HOWARD THURMAN

O SOVEREIGN LORD, MY STRONG DELIVERER,
WHO SHIELDS MY HEAD IN THE DAY OF BATTLE.
PSALM 140:7 NIV

Gus and Arthur were dressed in their overalls for the field. The call for breakfast was made, and they all gathered around the dining table with Father Berry at the head and Mother Nancy at the foot. John Berry could do very little reading, but he had memorized many passages of the Bible. He led the prayers on this Friday morning in mid-September in a manner usually reserved for Sunday mornings.

But this was a very special occasion. "Bow your heads please.

"Heavenly Father, we thank thee for this food and we ask a special blessing on our Son, Llewellyn, who is going off to school. Guide and protect him from hurt, harm and danger. Help him to learn his lessons well and bring him safely back to his family when school is over."

The family repeated the Lord's Prayer in unison and began to serve a delicious Sunday morning type breakfast.[25]

I Wouldn't Take Nothing for My Journey, LEONIDAS H. BERRY, M.D.

—⁄⁄⁄—

HEAL AND PROTECT

My mind is like a general, and my body is like an army.
I keep the body in shape and it does what I tell it to do.

HERSCHEL WALKER

YOU SHALL SERVE THE LORD YOUR GOD;
HE SHALL BLESS YOUR BREAD AND WATER,
AND I WILL TAKE SICKNESS FROM YOUR MIDST.

EXODUS 23:25 AMP

One day at the height of the yellow fever plague of St. Mary's, "Doc" Henry arose about 4 A.M. to get out the rig for a heavy day with Dr. Thomas. It was a very dark, cold and dreary night when he spotted some moving lights a good distance away in the area of the white folks' graveyard.

At first he paid little attention, but he began to hear distant noises like the howling of wolves. Suddenly he remembered that on the day before, they had buried "mean massa, Big Jim Milburn," who had dropsy for years and was stricken with the yellow plague. They had given him up for dead when he sat straight up; rolled his yellow eyes and sneezed. It was several hours later that he appeared really dead and he was hauled away for burial.

Henry was a deeply religious man and never believed in "haints"[Note: "haunts" or ghosts]—that is, never before this early morning experience. He aroused everybody in the cabin and pointed out the first real "haint" he had ever seen. Big Massa Jim had refused to die and was holding a "pow wow" with the other dead slave masters refusing to stay in hell. Others who had gathered around agreed with Doc Henry that it was time to sing and pray cause "massa Jim" and other "massas" was coming back.

The cabin group was led in prayer by Doc Henry:

"Oh God," intoned Brother Henry as he knelt on the dirt floor, "bow our heds belo' our hearts and our hearts belo' our knees, and our knees in some lonesum valley. Dear Lord, please God, tak' away dis plague, but don't bring back dem what's dead. Don't let dem massas stir up no more er dat yella potion."

With the aid of the kerosene lamp and with one eye open, Brother Henry looked at his yellow, bile-stained hands as they partially covered his face in prayer.

"I smells dat strong bitter gall, Lord, what dey's makin' up over dare, way over here, dear Lord. We have sinned agin you, Lord, but dere's moe sin agin us now dan we can bear. Protect us, your servants, Lord, and when we's dun wit dis world, take us in yo

*kingdom, massa Lord, where we will praise your name forever,
Amen. Amen. Amen."*

Up from their knees, the small group began to sing one of "de white folks' funeral songs," "Nearer My God to Thee." As they looked outside, they saw the beginning of the break of dawn. The peculiar lights in the graveyard were still moving, but now they could see human forms. They ventured out of the cabin and moved slowly toward the spectacle. Now there was a little more light, and they could see that the lights were coming from lanterns and suddenly beheld not slave masters rising from the dead, but slave workmen digging graves for dozens of slave masters and would-be slave masters.[24]

I Wouldn't Take Nothing for My Journey, Leonidas H. Berry, M.D.

—⁓—

"Grant Me Active Days of Peace and Truth"

*A little learning, indeed, may be a dangerous thing,
but the want of learning is a calamity to any people.*

Frederick Douglass

SHOW ME THE PATH WHERE I SHOULD WALK, O LORD;
POINT OUT THE RIGHT ROAD FOR ME TO FOLLOW. LEAD ME
BY YOUR TRUTH AND TEACH ME, FOR YOU ARE THE GOD
WHO SAVES ME. ALL DAY LONG I PUT MY HOPE IN YOU.

PSALM 25:4-5 NLT

Teach me, O Lord, the secret errors of my way,
Teach me the paths wherein I go astray,
Learn me the way to teach the word of love,
For that's the pure intelligence above.
As well as learning, give me that truth forever—
Which a mere worldly tie can never sever,
For though our bodies die, our souls will live forever,
To cultivate in every youthful mind,
Habitual grace, and sentiments refined.
Thus while I strive to govern human heart,
May I the heavenly precepts still impart;
Oh! may each youthful bosom, catch the sacred fire,
And youthful mind to virtues throne aspire.
Now fifteen years their destined course have run,
In fast succession round the central sun;
How did the follies of that period pass,
I ask myself—are they inscribed in brass?
Oh! Recollection, speed their fresh return,

And sure 'tis mine to be ashamed and mourn.

"What shall I ask, or what refrain to say?

Where shall I point, or how conclude my lay?

So much my weakness needs—so oft Thy voice,

Assures that weakness, and confirms my choice.

Oh, grant me active days of peace and truth,

Strength to my heart, and wisdom to my youth,

A sphere of usefulness—a soul to fill

That sphere with duty, and perform Thy will."

ANN PLATO, *Essays Including Biographies and Miscellaneous Pieces in Prose and Poetry*, HARTFORD, 1841.

—m—

"MY CUP OF JOY OVERFLOWS"

*Without God, all of our efforts turn to ashes
and our sunrise into the darkest of nights.
Without him, life is a meaningless drama
in which the decisive scenes are missing.*

MARTIN LUTHER KING JR.

Soul Cry

Gracious Savior, let me make,
Neither error or mistake—
Let me in Thy love abide,
Ever near Thy riven side.

Let me, counting all things dross,
Find my glory in the Cross;
Let me daily with Thee talk,
In Thy footsteps daily walk.

I would gladly follow Thee,
For Thou gently leadest me,
Where the pastures green doth grow,
Where the waters stillest flow.

For me is Thy table spread,
And Thou doth anoint my head,
And my cup of joy o'erflows
In the presence of my foes.

JOSEPHINE HENDERSON HERD, 1890

"MILLET! COME!"

It is better for us to succeed, though some die,
than for us to fail though all live.

WILLIAM PICKENS

THEN HE WILL FILL YOUR BARNS WITH GRAIN, AND
YOUR VATS WILL OVERFLOW WITH THE FINEST WINE.

PROVERBS 3:10 NLT

Oh God! Receive the morning greetings!
Ancestors! Receive the morning greetings!
We are here on the chosen day,
We are going to sow the seed,
We are going out to cultivate.
Oh God! Cause the millet to germinate,
Make the eight seeds sprout,
And the ninth calabash.

Give a wife to him who has none!
And to him who has a wife without children
Give a child!
Protect the men against thorns,

Against snake-bites,

Against ill winds!

Pour out the rain,

As we our water from a pot!

Millet! Come!

A Dogon Greeting to God at Sowing Time

—m—

CHILDREN WHO HONOR GOD

You are the product of the love and affection of
your parents, and throughout your life you have
drawn strength and hope from that love and security.

NELSON MANDELA

THE LORD PROTECTS THE FOREIGNERS AMONG US.
HE CARES FOR THE ORPHANS AND WIDOWS,
BUT HE FRUSTRATES THE PLANS OF THE WICKED.

PSALM 146:9 NLT

Oh my Gracious Preserver, Hitherto You have brought me. Be pleased when You bring me to childbirth to give me strength to bring forth living and perfect a being who shall be greatly instrumental in promoting Your glory. Though conceived in sin and brought forth in iniquity, yet Your infinite wisdom can bring a clean thing out of an unclean; a vessel of honor filled for Your glory. Grant me to live a life of gratitude to You for Your innumerable benefits. O Lord my God, instruct my ignorance and enlighten my Darkness. You are my King. Take the entire possession of my powers and faculties and let me be no longer under the dominion of sin. Give me a sincere and hearty repentance for all my offenses and strengthen by Your grace my resolutions on amendment and circumspection for the time to come. Grant me also the spirit of Prayer and Supplication according to Your own most gracious promises.

PHILLIS WHEATLEY

—⚡—

"I HEAR THY VOICE"

I believe I have had a glimpse of God many times.
I believe because believing is believable, and
no one can prove it unbelievable.

DUKE ELLINGTON

Soul Cry

I hear Thy voice, Oh God of grace,
That loudly calls for me;
That I may rise and feel Thy face,
Before the dawning day.

While others still lie in their beds,
And have not thought to pray,
Their sleep doth still keep them secure,
Like death, upon the frame.

But, O my God, 'tis Thou that hears
My mourning feeble cries;
I cry for grace, Thy Spirit's aid,
Before the sun do rise.

That like the sun I may fulfil,
My business of the day;
To give the life that Jesus did,
To go and preach today.

O like the sun I would fulfil,

My duties and obey;

Thy Spirit's voice that speaks within,

And tells me keep the day.

JOHN JEA, 1816

LIFE-CHANGING PRAYERS FOR YOUR DAILY NEEDS

BOLDNESS

Courage is one step ahead of fear.

COLEMAN YOUNG

AFTER THIS PRAYER, THE BUILDING WHERE THEY WERE MEETING
SHOOK, AND THEY WERE ALL FILLED WITH THE HOLY SPIRIT.
AND THEY PREACHED GOD'S MESSAGE WITH BOLDNESS.

ACTS 4:31 NLT

Gracious Father,

By invitation You have given me exclusive access to You and
said that I can talk with You anytime I want. So I am taking
advantage of that offer today as I seek Your help in dealing with a
matter on my job.

I know that not everyone has the same love for You as I do, and
I understand when some are not so receptive if I try and talk with
them about You. Your Scriptures say that, as Christians, we will
sometimes be persecuted for standing up for the Gospel. But being
rejected hurts. Sometimes it even causes me to fear—to shy away

and not even try to share Your love with others, though I want to very badly.

You remind me that the fear I sometimes feel does not come from You. So I trust You to give me the courage to take my stand and boldly speak about You no matter how people react. Your promise is that You will always be with me, and I take comfort in knowing that I am never alone. You will tell me just what to say. Amen.

—⟋⟍—

CHILDREN

Our children's allegiance to high goals and standards
will be principally established and enforced,
not on the campus, but in the home.

HARRY EDWARDS

TRAIN A CHILD IN THE WAY HE SHOULD GO,
AND WHEN HE IS OLD HE WILL NOT TURN FROM IT.

PROVERBS 22:6 NIV

Soul Cry

Dear Father,

We still get excited just thinking about the births of our children. You gave us joy and excitement with each one. But now, as we watch them enter their teenage years, we can feel that joy and excitement turning into concern.

We know that You have great plans for our children. As parents we are responsible to make sure they stay on the right path so that Your plans for them will happen. But there are so many evil influences in the world today. How do we protect them from the evil trappings of the enemy? How do we make sure they stay focused and do not yield to temptations to do wrong?

We cannot be with our children all the time. But we are encouraged in knowing that You are always watching over them. When they are tempted to make wrong decisions, Your Holy Spirit prompts them to do right. And when others plot and scheme against them, You make whatever evil is turned toward them work together for their good.

Thank You for giving us godly wisdom as we continue to teach and train our children. We arm ourselves with Your Word, and we pray and intercede for them just as Jesus Christ prays and intercedes for us. Amen.

—⁕—

DIFFICULT RELATIONSHIPS

True peace is not merely the absence of tensions;
it is the presence of justice.

MARTIN LUTHER KING JR.

MAKE EVERY EFFORT TO LIVE IN PEACE
WITH ALL MEN AND TO BE HOLY.

HEBREWS 12:14 NIV

Holy Father,

The world's answer to dealing with offense is usually to retaliate or try to get even. And at times, that's exactly how I feel. But I realize that fighting back is not the way to mend a broken relationship. It only makes things worse.

Your Word says that You always responded to persecution with love—holding Your peace no matter how badly You were treated. That takes a lot of strength. I can see by Your action that it is more important for me to be a peacemaker than to try to defend myself.

I am glad that I have Your Spirit inside me. It is the presence of the Holy Spirit that makes me want to be just like You—to respond to persecution in the same way as You. I can't say that offense does not hurt, because it does. But I know that with Your help I can handle it.

Thank You for being such a loving God, and for allowing me to draw from Your strength when mine alone just won't hold up. Amen.

—◆—

DISAPPOINTMENT

Disappointment drives men to desperate lengths.

MARTIN LUTHER KING JR.

"HAVE I NOT COMMANDED YOU? BE STRONG AND COURAGEOUS. DO NOT BE TERRIFIED; DO NOT BE DISCOURAGED, FOR THE LORD YOUR GOD WILL BE WITH YOU WHEREVER YOU GO."

JOSHUA 1:9 NIV

Almighty God,

Once again, something that I was hoping for so much has not come. Truthfully, I am hurt and disappointed. But the more I think about it, I realize that perhaps this was not what You wanted for me in the first place.

There is nothing wrong with planning and making preparation. In fact, You encourage it. But I was wrong to assume that just because the idea sounded good it was what You wanted for me. I'm sorry for being so presumptuous. Sometimes I get excited when something attracts me. It's easy for me to think, *That's what I'm supposed to do!* or *I would really be good at that.* But I acknowledge that You know what's best for me. Your Word says You have mapped out a plan for my life and are ordering my footsteps along that path. What I think and what I want out of life pale in the sight of the things that You have in store for me.

What an awesome God You are to take time out and give me special attention. Knowing how much You care about me and my future, I refuse to be disappointed when things don't go the way I think they should. I know there's a better plan, because my wise and loving God is watching out for me. Amen.

—⟋⟍—

EMPLOYMENT

A man is worked upon by what he works on.
He may carve out his circumstances,
but his circumstances will carve him out as well.

FREDERICK DOUGLASS

MAKE IT YOUR AMBITION TO LEAD A QUIET LIFE,
TO MIND YOUR OWN BUSINESS AND TO WORK WITH
YOUR HANDS, JUST AS WE TOLD YOU, SO THAT YOUR
DAILY LIFE MAY WIN THE RESPECT OF OUTSIDERS AND
SO THAT YOU WILL NOT BE DEPENDENT ON ANYBODY.

1 THESSALONIANS 4:11-12 NIV

Heavenly Father,

I have a strong sense of responsibility when it comes to caring
for my family, and I know that pleases You. That's why I am asking
for Your help as I decide which job will best help me do that.

In addition to Your command that I provide for my family, You
have said the only thing I should owe any man is love. Sure, it
would be nice to make so much money that I never had to be

concerned about paying bills or giving my family the things that they need and desire. But I cannot let money be the sole reason for accepting a position.

I believe that as I am obedient to You, as I live honorably and am responsible in the way I conduct my affairs, You will see to it that my needs are met. By Your Spirit You will direct my steps so that I know that I have made the right decision—one that will benefit my family and me in the best possible way.

You promised to bless the work of my hands, so in advance I praise and thank You for success at whichever job I select. I ask for wisdom and knowledge to make wise decisions and for skill and creativity to enhance the ordinary and learn new things. And I thank You for giving me wisdom to make decisions that I can be comfortable with and that please You. Amen.

—⟋⟍—

FAITH

Living on faith is a mental exercise.

SUSAN TAYLOR

FOR WE WALK BY FAITH [WE REGULATE OUR LIVES
AND CONDUCT OURSELVES BY OUR CONVICTION OR BELIEF
RESPECTING MAN'S RELATIONSHIP TO GOD AND DIVINE THINGS,
WITH TRUST AND HOLY FERVOR; THUS WE WALK]
NOT BY SIGHT OR APPEARANCE.

2 CORINTHIANS 5:7 AMP

Ever-Present Father,

Abraham was called the "Father of Faith," yet there were times in his life when it seemed faith would have been the furthest thing from his mind.

I think about the strong faith of Abraham sometimes when things in my own life are going so rough that I can see no way out. How could Abraham believe and trust in a God he could not see, hear, or touch? How can I?

Abraham believed in You despite the fact that You were not present in the flesh. Your word was enough to convince him of Your love for him, and that You would do whatever You promised.

I don't know if my faith is as strong as Abraham's, but I do believe Your word. I also believe that You love me just as much as You loved him. I don't need to see You to believe that You are with me—watching over me and taking care of me. And I don't need to hear Your voice to know that You heard my cry and will answer me. I sense Your presence every time I pray.

For me, Your promise that You will never leave me or forsake me is more than enough.

Amen!

FINANCES

*At the bottom of education, at the bottom of politics, even at
the bottom of religion, there must be economic independence.*

BOOKER T. WASHINGTON

THIS SAME GOD WHO TAKES CARE OF ME WILL
SUPPLY ALL YOUR NEEDS FROM HIS GLORIOUS RICHES,
WHICH HAVE BEEN GIVEN TO US IN CHRIST JESUS.

PHILIPPIANS 4:19 NLT

God, My Provider,

Everything belongs to You. And Your desire for me is that I
have everything I need to be healthy and successful. That's why I
have peace in knowing I can count on You for help with my
financial needs.

If I based my financial status on what my bank account looked
like, I would surely be on the losing end. But thanks to You I don't
have to go by what I have. I don't even have to depend on a pay
raise to know that I will be OK. I have Your promise that You will
meet every need I have according to Your riches in Christ Jesus. You

have all the resources to do just that, because the earth and everything that fills it belongs to You. That includes houses and lands, food and clothing—even money.

I take joy in knowing that just as you care for the birds, the flowers, and the trees, You also care for me. I will faithfully obey Your Word that tells me to tithe and give generously, and I will not be concerned about my own needs. I am confident You will fulfill Your promise to take care of me. Amen.

—⁓—

FRIENDSHIP

People see God every day; they just don't recognize him.

PEARL BAILEY

YOU WILL FIND HIM IF YOU SEEK HIM WITH ALL YOUR HEART.

DEUTERONOMY 4:29 NKJV

Heavenly Father,

It is easy to describe someone whom you're close to as a "friend." But when it comes to true friendship, I am convinced that there is no friend like You.

From the day I called You Lord, You have never failed me. You have always been right there—to listen to my problems, heal my hurts, provide me comfort or correction whenever I needed it. Never have You talked about me behind my back, looked down on me, rejected or disappointed me.

I don't find those qualities among some who call me friend. There have been times when even those who are very close to me have let me down. I cannot count on others like I can count on You. It hurts, and I am disappointed. But I remember how You responded when Judas betrayed You. You called him friend.

Your Word says if we are to have friends we must first be friendly. I love people, so I will continue to look for new friendships. But I put my trust in You, and not people.

You have called me friend. What an honor! Amen.

—m—

GRACE

One endures with patience the pain
in the other fellow's stomach.
JOAQUIM MACHADO DE ASSIS

"MY YOKE FITS PERFECTLY, AND
THE BURDEN I GIVE YOU IS LIGHT."
MATTHEW 11:30 NLT

Heavenly Father,

Sometimes it really does feel like the weight of the world is on my shoulders. I don't want all of this responsibility, yet it has been given to me.

At first, I wanted to say, "Why me?" And to be honest, it was because I was afraid that I would fail. But when I look around and see what others are faced with, I have to ask myself, *Why not me?*

Obviously, You trust me to do a good job; otherwise, I don't believe You would allow such a heavy burden to be placed on me. And if I were to fail, I know that You would be the first to understand and forgive me.

I know You care for me, and You know what affects me. So, I trust You to help me through this trying time. You promised to take care of my problems as I cast them over on You. So I am confident that I am not alone in this situation. Even the weight of this matter is no problem. I confess that I am not strong enough to bear it, but You are.

You always know exactly how much I can bear, and I thank You for always being there to lighten the load. Amen.

—◊◊◊—

GUIDANCE

I was advised to "go and try" physics because in the words of one counselor, "You're good enough."

RON MCNAIR

THE LORD'S PLANS STAND FIRM FOREVER;
HIS INTENTIONS CAN NEVER BE SHAKEN.

PSALM 33:11 NLT

Heavenly Father,

It is so easy to get caught up in trying to please people. Sometimes this results in making the wrong decision. That's why I come to You for help with making this important decision. Truly, I don't know which way to go.

If I base my decision on what I think, I could mess things up. You, on the other hand, are never wrong. Your Word is sure, and Your promises never fail. So I can trust that whatever You say is right.

As I pray, I am confident that You are standing ready to help. On the inside, I can hear Your voice beckoning, "Follow Me." That is so consistent with Your Word, which says I can put my trust in You and look expectantly for You to show me the way.

My understanding of this matter is not as deep as Yours. You know all things and can see much further than I can. So right now I roll this care over onto You, expecting that I will receive the direction I need to make the right decision. Thank You, Father, for leading me. Amen.

HEALING

Good health is a duty to yourself, to your contemporaries,
to your inheritors, to the progress of the world.

GWENDOLYN BROOKS

JESUS WENT THROUGH ALL THE TOWNS AND VILLAGES, TEACHING
IN THEIR SYNAGOGUES, PREACHING THE GOOD NEWS OF THE
KINGDOM AND HEALING EVERY DISEASE AND SICKNESS.

MATTHEW 9:35 NIV

Heavenly Father,

My body has been attacked with sickness, and symptoms are
causing me discomfort and hindering me from functioning as I
should. As I look back over my life, it's easy to figure out that much
of what I am dealing with is my own fault because I have not given
proper care to my body.

But I am encouraged that Your Word says I am healed and
made whole by the stripes that wounded Christ Jesus—not just in
my spirit but my body as well. I am so grateful that He was

willing to be crucified for me and that He understands my pain and suffering.

You have said that Your Word is medicine and life to my flesh and it will heal and deliver me. You never lie, and Your Word will accomplish what You sent it to do because You have promised that it will never fail. This sickness is a weapon against me to keep me from doing the work that You have assigned to me. But it is not too hard or impossible for You to heal.

I am comforted because of Your presence and promise to never leave me. And I trust You to deliver me and make this work for my good just as You have said. Please give me strength and patience while I wait for my body to mend. And help me to use wisdom in giving proper care to my body in the future. Amen.

—m—

HEALTH

Health is a human right, not a privilege to be purchased.
SHIRLEY CHISHOLM

DEAR FRIEND, I AM PRAYING THAT ALL IS WELL WITH YOU AND
THAT YOUR BODY IS AS HEALTHY AS I KNOW YOUR SOUL IS.
3 JOHN 1:2 NLT

Heavenly Father,

Thank You for doctors who are dedicated to our well-being, but
I know I am not alone when I say I do not like being sick and having
to go to one. Now that I am sick, I realize just how important it is to
maintain a healthy body.

First, I ask Your forgiveness for not always being responsive to
the signals my body was sending. I could have been more attentive,
but instead I took my good health for granted. Now, in part because
of my negligence, I am paying the price through sickness.

I am glad that Jesus paid an even greater price when He gave
His life on the Cross for my sickness and disease. Because of His
sacrifice, healing has already been provided for me.

I confess my wrong and believe I am healed by His stripes. I also receive healing for my mind, and I purpose to listen more attentively when my body is speaking to me. Truly, it is Your desire that I walk in health, both body and soul. Thank You, Father, for healing me today. Amen.

—⫘—

LEADERSHIP

I do not wish to secure any job from the President of the United States or anybody else that can give political favors. A leader of the masses must be free to obey and follow the interests of the masses.

A. PHILIP RANDOLPH

WHEREVER YOU ASSEMBLE,
I WANT MEN TO PRAY WITH HOLY HANDS LIFTED
UP TO GOD, FREE FROM ANGER AND CONTROVERSY.

I TIMOTHY 2:8 NLT

Lord God,

This is a great country we live in. But it would not be such a great place to live were it not for You and the godly leaders You place in authority—men and women who have Your heart and are determined to obey You.

These are the people who daily make decisions that affect me and my family, and the entire Body of Christ as we dwell in this land. It is only by and through Your leadership and guidance that they are able to make right decisions. So I pray and ask that You give them wisdom and help them to be free to hear from You and obey Your instructions.

You perfect those things that concern us and make them work together for our good. Therefore, I am assured that today this country is a good place to dwell because its leaders follow after You. I also pray that whatever they are lacking, You will give it to them as they seek You. When it comes time to take a stand for right, they will be people of integrity. They will not be ashamed of You or Your Word.

Thank You for this great land and the great leaders You have given to us. Amen.

—◊◊◊—

LONELINESS

We live amid swarms of people, yet there is a vast distance
between people, a distance that words cannot bridge.

RICHARD WRIGHT

"I WILL BE WITH YOU CONSTANTLY UNTIL I HAVE FINISHED
GIVING YOU EVERYTHING I HAVE PROMISED."

GENESIS 28:15 NLT

Almighty God,

Sitting here staring out the window, for a moment I caught a
vision of the little boy in a movie I saw who was accidentally left
behind at home alone while his family went off on vacation. All of a
sudden, I knew what it was like to be "home alone." No one to talk
to; nowhere to go. It's a terrible feeling of being cut off—
disconnected from family and friends.

But then I remembered You. My Father! And I immediately
began to feel the comfort of Your presence. And I realized that I am
never alone because You and I are connected. Like a tree, You are the
vine and I am a healthy branch—firmly connected and growing
stronger every day. I heard Your voice in my spirit saying, "Seek

and you will find; knock and the door will be opened to you"
(MATTHEW 7:7 NIV).

It's nice to have company. But that old saying, "Silence is
golden," also has a lot of meaning. There are times when I need to be
alone with You—to be still so I can hear Your voice in my heart. It is
during those quiet times that I can find true peace, joy, and comfort.

You promised never to leave me alone. Because You watch over
Your Word to always do what You say, I can never be lonely. Amen.

—∾—

LOVE

Love stretches your heart and makes you big inside.
MARGARET WALKER

AND THIS I PRAY: THAT YOUR LOVE MAY ABOUND
YET MORE AND MORE AND EXTEND TO ITS FULLEST
DEVELOPMENT IN KNOWLEDGE AND ALL KEEN INSIGHT
[THAT YOUR LOVE MAY DISPLAY ITSELF IN GREATER DEPTH OF
ACQUAINTANCE AND MORE COMPREHENSIVE DISCERNMENT], SO

Soul Cry

THAT YOU MAY SURELY LEARN TO SENSE WHAT IS VITAL, AND
APPROVE AND PRIZE WHAT IS EXCELLENT AND OF REAL VALUE.

PHILIPPIANS 1:9-10 AMP

Father of Love,

From the world's perception, love is a simple thing. That's because they don't understand the true concept of love.

Love is not wrapped up in feelings. Those kinds of emotions come and go. But real love—the God kind of love—endures all things. Like You, love is everlasting.

As I begin to understand You better, I begin to know what true love is all about. I understand what it means to love my neighbor as myself. I know the importance of loving those who despise and persecute me. And I understand from my heart the sacrifice Jesus made by giving His life for me.

Your Word is filled with examples of love—true love—and how it should be applied in our lives. But You are the perfect example. You created me out of a love and desire for fellowship. Your Son, Jesus, even gave His own life as a sacrifice so that the love relationship between You and me could be preserved.

Because I have Your love, as a good soldier I am able to endure hardships such as persecution, abuse, and unkind attitudes. The love of God on the inside helps me to overcome those things, and it gives me peace, joy, and comfort.

I base my life on love. Thank You, Father, for putting Your love in my heart. Amen.

—⁂—

MARRIAGE

One of the realities after years of marriage is that whatever changes you had planned to make for that person are going to happen slowly or not happen at all.

BILL COSBY

GIVE HONOR TO MARRIAGE, AND REMAIN FAITHFUL
TO ONE ANOTHER IN MARRIAGE.

HEBREWS 13:4 NLT

Gracious Father,

Whatever happened to the sanctity of marriage?

Since the beginning of time, when you provided Adam with a wife and called her Eve, You have been concerned about the relationship between husband and wife. It's too bad that many people don't share Your feelings. To them marriage is a joke. They try it, and if they don't like it they quit.

I am glad that my spouse and I recognize the sanctity of our marriage, and we pledge never to do anything that might violate that sacred trust we share. Sure, there are times when we disagree. There are even times when we may get upset or angry with each other. But no disagreement or anger is worth jeopardizing this great relationship You have created between us.

We believe we both found that "good thing" in all the earth that You handpicked and reserved expressly for each of us. While we pray for other marriages, and even for those planning to be married, help us to work hard at keeping our marriage fresh and exciting. Show us new ways to enjoy each other as we spend quality time together. And show us how to keep alive the love You have given us, as we respect and honor each other and You.

Thanks to You, Lord, ours is a marriage made in heaven. Amen.

—⟋⟍—

Purpose

There is a Purpose that invades all his purposes
and a Wisdom that invades all his wisdoms.

HOWARD THURMAN

I KNOW THE THOUGHTS AND PLANS THAT I HAVE
FOR YOU, SAYS THE LORD, THOUGHTS AND PLANS
FOR WELFARE AND PEACE AND NOT FOR EVIL,
TO GIVE YOU HOPE IN YOUR FINAL OUTCOME.

JEREMIAH 29:11 AMP

Father God,

Why am I here? I've asked myself this question many times,
only to settle on the same answer. I am here because of You—
because of Your great love for me and the plans You have
established for me that will lead to my success.

I am here to worship You and to bring glory to You by the life
that I live. And I am here to share Your love with all of mankind.

Because You made me, I am not foreign to You. Neither are my
thoughts. Sometimes I'm sure my thoughts don't line up with Yours,

and my plans are probably miles away from what You have in store for me. Understanding that, and knowing that Your plans are exceedingly greater and will take me farther than I could ever imagine, I purpose to commit my life and my works to You.

Your Word has become wisdom to me, so I use it in my daily walk—submitting to it so that I can know with assurance that I am living in a way that pleases You and brings You glory. It also guarantees that I will succeed at whatever I do.

Your promise is never to leave me alone. I am comforted today in knowing You are always with me—abiding in me as I abide in You. With You on my side I have no reason to fear or be concerned. You have become a shield and protection, my present and my future. Amen.

—〰—

SADNESS

We gather strength from sadness and from pain.
Each time we die we learn to live again.

ANONYMOUS

HE HEALS THE BROKENHEARTED AND BINDS UP THEIR WOUNDS
[CURING THEIR PAINS AND THEIR SORROWS].

PSALM 147:3 AMP

Dear Lord,

I've watched and prayed as others around me have worked through the pain of losing a loved one. But never did I imagine just how hurtful this could be until I experienced it personally.

How does one prepare for such a loss? How can life go on when someone you shared so much with is no longer a part of your life?

Father, it is hard. The pain is too much for me to bear alone. I must rely on You and Your strength to help me through it. Jesus knew that same sadness when His friend Lazarus died. However, through faith in You, Jesus knew He would see His friend again.

You remind me that You are fully aware of my thoughts and feelings, and that I don't have to bear this burden alone. I look to You now for comfort.

Your Word says sorrow is better than laughter, for by the sadness of the countenance the heart is made better. It is a sad time now, I know. But I also know that joy always comes again. Thank You for giving me Your joy. Amen.

—~m~—

STRESS

Oppression does not always crush the spirit of progress.
Men will achieve in spite of it.

CARTER G. WOODSON

"COME TO ME, ALL YOU WHO ARE WEARY AND
BURDENED, AND I WILL GIVE YOU REST."

MATTHEW 11:28 NIV

Father God,

When I took on this project, I was sure I would have the time to devote to it. I never took the time to look at all the other things that were demanding my time. And now I am stretched so far that I feel I cannot be affective in *any* area. If I don't get a handle on things quickly, I'm afraid I will crumble.

You encourage me to be still and realize that You are God. You are my helper, and You are my strength. So I have no reason to fear or get stressed out over what to You is a simple thing to fix.

I ask You to help me to prioritize according to its importance everything that is before me. If I do not need to be involved in a particular project, give me peace to accept that and cut it loose. Then, help me to be faithful to that which remains so that I can represent You well in my service.

Finally, I know there are those who will take unfair advantage of my generosity. Help me to know when to say "yes" to accepting a project, and also give me the boldness to graciously decline others. Amen.

TEMPTATION

*A man must live in this world and work out
his own salvation in the midst of temptation.*

FRANK YERBY

"KEEP WATCHING AND PRAYING THAT YOU MAY
NOT ENTER INTO TEMPTATION; THE SPIRIT
IS WILLING, BUT THE FLESH IS WEAK."

MATTHEW 26:41 NASB

Dear Lord,

The fact that You would put the word "temptation" in the same
sentence with the word "evil" in Matthew 6:13 tells me that You are
serious in Your warning that I should avoid being tempted. It also
helps me to better understand why the enemy uses temptation as a
major tool to cause people to sin and keep them from serving You.

Everywhere you look, there is temptation. Sadly, it is often
disguised in the form of pleasurable things such as movies, music,
and video games, and people don't recognize it. To them it is just
good fun.

Your Word said that we are not ignorant when it comes to recognizing the tricks and schemes the devil lays out to destroy us. So, I am very watchful to make sure I don't do anything that would not please You or give him any opportunity to lead me astray.

Your Holy Spirit helps me to recognize those evil trappings. And Your Word, which I study daily, has become a weapon for me to use in fending off the temptation and the tempter. And if that is not enough, I have Your promise that You will provide a way for me to escape. Thank You for covering me. Amen.

—⁓—

THANKSGIVING

It is a dangerous thing to ask why someone else has been given more. It is humbling—and indeed healthy— to ask why you have been given so much.

CONDOLEEZA RICE

LET US COME BEFORE HIS PRESENCE WITH
THANKSGIVING; LET US MAKE A JOYFUL
NOISE TO HIM WITH SONGS OF PRAISE!

PSALM 95:2 AMP

Heavenly Father,

I have so much to be thankful for. You have proven over and over again just how much You love me as You met my needs, faithfully answered my prayers, and gave me the secret desires of my heart. Who on earth would be so gracious?

When I awaken in the morning, Yours is the precious face that I seek. And when I go to bed at night, it is Your sweet voice that lulls me to sleep. Your presence guides me during the day and guards me through the night, keeping me in perfect peace. You do not sleep, but instead are preparing blessings for me as I do. Whenever I need to talk, You're always ready to listen. You have already planned my future and prepared the steps for my success, so I place my hand in Yours and follow You.

Father, if I had the ability and strength to stand and name each of my blessings, I believe that I would be standing throughout eternity. But, should I become presumptuous, please forgive me and help me to always say, "Thank You, Lord!" Amen.

TRAGEDY

I've had tragedy, but I have had lots of joy and triumph.

<small>CORETTA SCOTT KING</small>

WHEN YOU GO THROUGH THE DEEP WATERS AND
GREAT TROUBLE, I WILL BE WITH YOU. WHEN YOU
GO THROUGH RIVERS OF DIFFICULTY, YOU WILL NOT DROWN!
WHEN YOU WALK THROUGH THE FIRE OF OPPRESSION,
YOU WILL NOT BE BURNED UP; THE FLAMES WILL NOT
CONSUME YOU. FOR I AM THE LORD, YOUR GOD,
THE HOLY ONE OF ISRAEL, YOUR SAVIOR.

<small>ISAIAH 43:2-3 NLT</small>

Heavenly Father,

No one can ever know the true meaning of the words "tragedy struck home" until tragedy really does hit them or their family. I now know firsthand, because it has happened to us. My first reaction was fear. And then there was a strong feeling of helplessness because I realized there was nothing I could do.

I am angry because I know that this is an outright attack from the devil, whose sole purpose is to steal, kill, and destroy. But I am glad I can come to You—the Giver of life—and ask Your help as our family pulls together to support one another through this difficult time.

Your Word says You give us life in abundance, and Your promise is Your presence and Your peace. I refuse to let fear get a grip on me. I know You can help us. You are the only true God—the Maker of Heaven and earth and all there is. No thing on earth is a challenge for You—not even these tragic circumstances.

You have promised strength, Your help, even in some cases redemption of all I've lost, and a final, satisfying resolution to my pain when I come home to You. I take joy in knowing that while I don't feel so strong right now, You are being strong for my family and me. Father, thank You for loving us so much. My trust is in You. Amen.

—␣—

THE LORD'S PRAYER

Behold, the only thing greater than yourself.

ALEX HALEY

YOU HAVE BEEN SO KIND TO ME AND SAVED MY LIFE,
AND YOU HAVE GRANTED ME SUCH MERCY.

GENESIS 19:19 NLT

Our Father which art in heaven,
Hallowed be thy name.
Thy kingdom come.
Thy will be done in earth, as it is in heaven.
Give us this day our daily bread.
And forgive us our debts,
as we forgive our debtors.
And lead us not into temptation,
but deliver us from evil:
For thine is the kingdom, and the power,
and the glory, forever.
Amen.

MATTHEW 6:9-13 KJV

Acknowledgements

1   Katherine Dunham in "She Danced to Teach—And They Loved It", *American Visions*, February 1987.

2   Jacob Stroyer, *My Life in the South*, New and Enlarged Edition. Salem: Salem Observer Book and Job Print. 1885, 1898, p. 24.

3   *Conversations with God: Two Centuries of Prayer by African-Americans* (1994), ed. James Melvin Washington. Harper Collins: New York.

4   *Morning Glories:* Second Edition, March 17, 1890-1901 (Atlanta, GA.: Franklin Printing and Publishing Co), 1901.

5   Marian Wright Edelman, *I'm Your Child, God: Prayers for Our Children*, Illustrated by Bryan Collier Hyperion Books for Children, October 2002.

6   Rev. Harold A. Carter, *The Prayer Tradition of Black People*, 1985.

7   Productions of Mrs. Maria W. Stewart, presented to the First African Baptist Church & Society, of the City of Boston, 1835, page 35.

8   Marian Wright Edelman, *Guide My Feet: Prayers and Meditations for Our Children*, Harper Colllins: New York.

9   Ibid.

[10] Richard Allen, *The Life Experiences and Gospel Labors of the Rt. Rev. Richard Allen.* pp. 25, 26.

[11] Marian Wright Edelman, *I'm Your Child, God: Prayers for Our Children,* Illustrated by Bryan Collier Hyperion Books for Children, October 2002.

[12] Charles Taylor, *The Black Church and Juneteenth.*

[13] Richard Allen, *The Life Experiences and Gospel Labors of the Rt. Rev. Richard Allen.* pp. 25, 26

[14] Ibid p. 27.

[15] Productions of Mrs. Maria W. Stewart, presented to the First African Baptist Church & Society, of the City of Boston, 1835, page 28.

[16] Ibid. p. 31.

[17] Harold A. Carter, *Prayer Tradition of Black People,* 1985.

[18] Ibid.

[19] Productions of Mrs. Maria W. Stewart, presented to the First African Baptist Church & Society, of the City of Boston, 1835, page 46.

[20] Josephine Henderson Heard, Morning Glories, Philadelphia, PA., 1890.

[21] Elose Alberta Veronica Bibb, *Poems by Elose Bibb,* 1895, The Monthly Review Press, 5 Park Sq., Boston, Mass.

[22] Leonidas H. Berry, MD, *I Wouldn't Take Nothing for My Journey*, published by Johnson Publishing Company, Inc., 1981—Fortress Monroe and Old Point Comfort, Va., p. 45.

[23] Ibid. p. 105.

[24] Ibid. p. 12,13.

Additional copies of this and other
Honor Books products are available
from your local bookseller.

*Soul Praise: Amazing Stories Behind the Great African
American Hymns and Negro Spirituals*

*God Has Soul: Celebrating the Indomitable Spirit of
African Americans*

*Voices of Hope: Timeless Expressions of Faith from
African Americans*

If you have enjoyed this book,
or if it has had an impact on your life,
we would like to hear from you.

Please contact us at:

Honor Books, Dept. 201
4050 Lee Vance View
Colorado Springs, CO 80918
Or visit our Web site:
www.cookministries.com

HONOR **HB** BOOKS

Inspiration and Motivation for the Seasons of Life